MAD
JACKPOT

WARNER BOOKS

A Warner Communications Company

WARNER BOOKS EDITION

Copyright © 1980, 1981, and 1989 by E.C. Publications, Inc.
All rights reserved.
No part of this book may be reproduced without permission.
For information address:
E.C. Publications, Inc.
485 Madison Avenue
New York, N.Y. 10022

**Title "MAD" used with permission of its owner,
E.C. Publications, Inc.**

This Warner Books Edition is published by
arrangement with E.C. Publications, Inc.

**Warner Books, Inc.
666 Fifth Avenue
New York, N.Y. 10103**

Ⓦ A Warner Communications Company

Printed in the United States of America

First Printing: February 1989

10   9   8   7   6   5   4   3   2   1

FLOPEYE

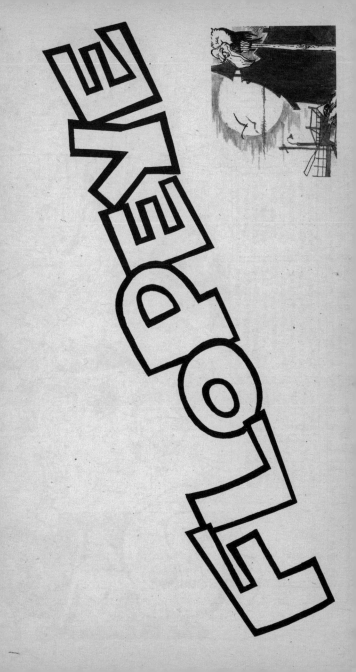

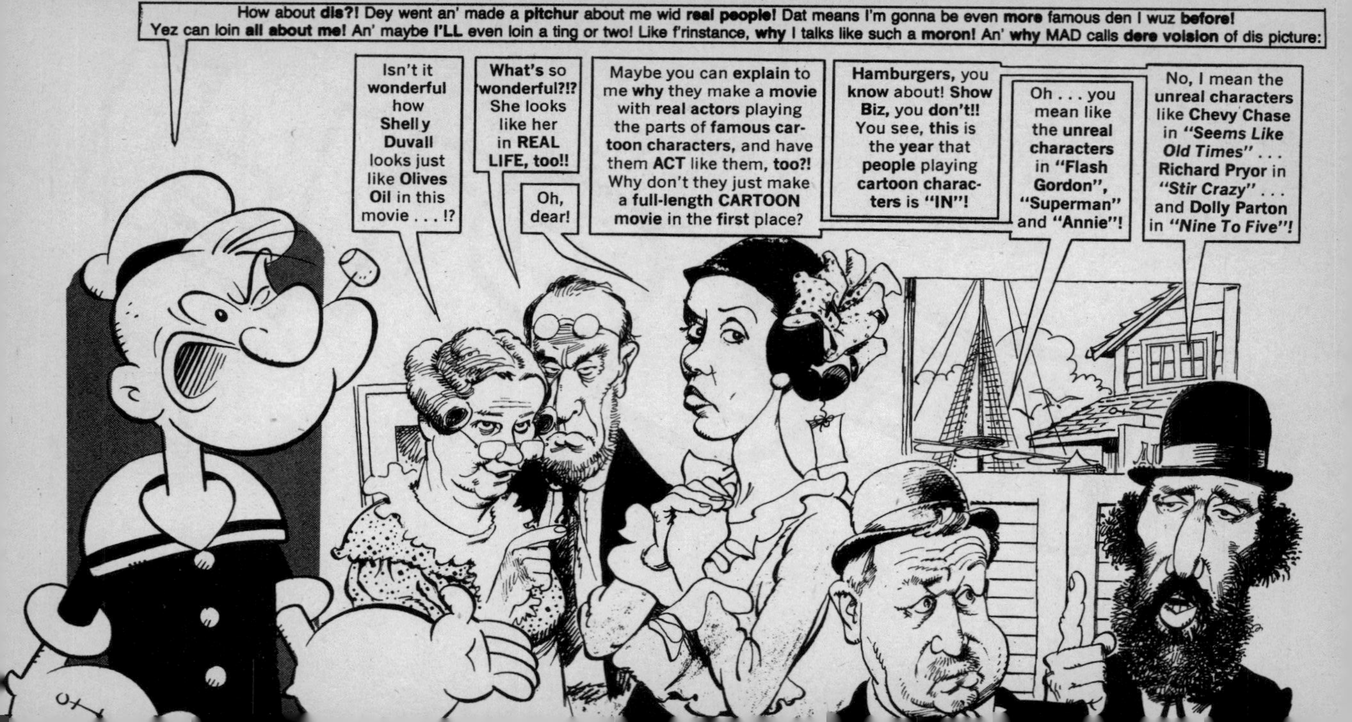
How about **dis?!** Dey went an' made a **pitchur** about me wid **real people!** Dat means I'm gonna be even **more** famous den I wuz **before!** Yez can loin **all about me!** An' maybe **I'LL** even loin a ting or two! Like f'rinstance, **why** I talks like such a **moron!** An' **why** MAD calls **dere volsion** of dis picture:
Isn't it **wonderful** how **Shelly Duvall** looks just like **Olives Oil** in this movie . . . !?
What's so **wonderful?!?** She looks like her in **REAL LIFE, too!!**
Oh, dear!
Maybe you can **explain** to me **why** they make a **movie** with **real actors** playing the parts of **famous cartoon characters,** and have them **ACT** like them, **too?!** Why don't they just make a **full-length CARTOON movie** in the **first** place?
Hamburgers, you **know** about! **Show Biz,** you **don't!!** You see, **this** is the **year** that **people** playing **cartoon characters** is **"IN"!**
Oh . . . you mean like the **unreal characters** in **"Flash Gordon", "Superman"** and **"Annie"!**
No, I mean the **unreal characters** like **Chevy Chase** in ***"Seems Like Old Times"*** . . . **Richard Pryor** in ***"Stir Crazy"*** . . . and **Dolly Parton** in ***"Nine To Five"!***

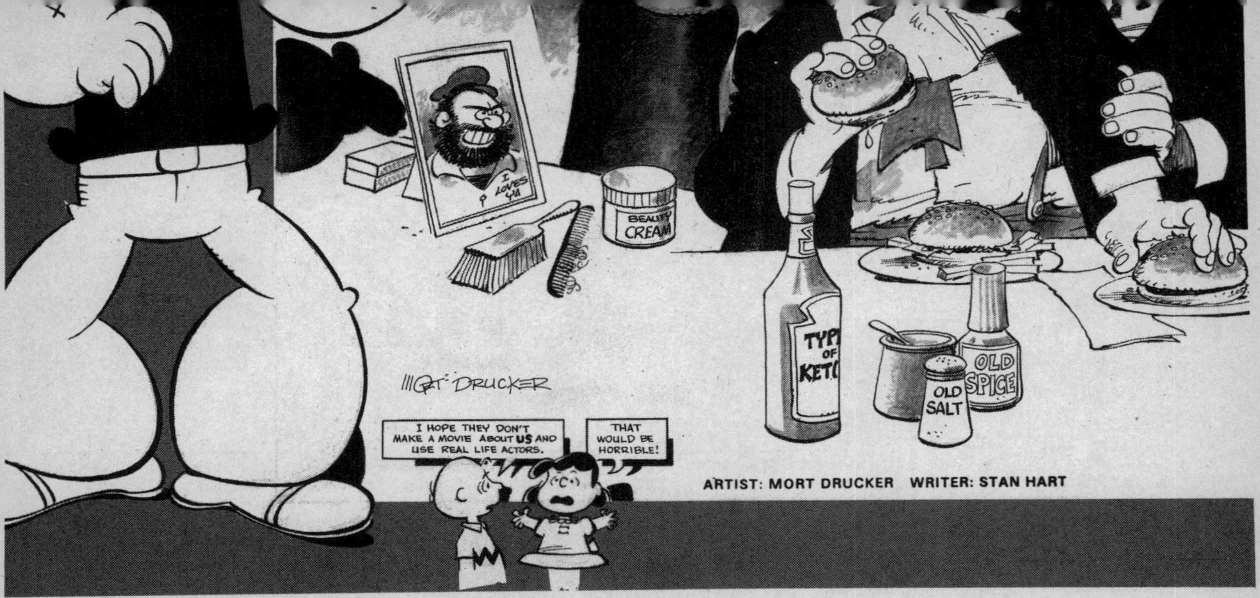
I LOVES YA
BEAUTY CREAM
TYPE OF KETC
OLD SPICE
OLD SALT
MORT DRUCKER
I HOPE THEY DON'T MAKE A MOVIE ABOUT US AND USE REAL LIFE ACTORS.
THAT WOULD BE HORRIBLE!

ARTIST: MORT DRUCKER WRITER: STAN HART

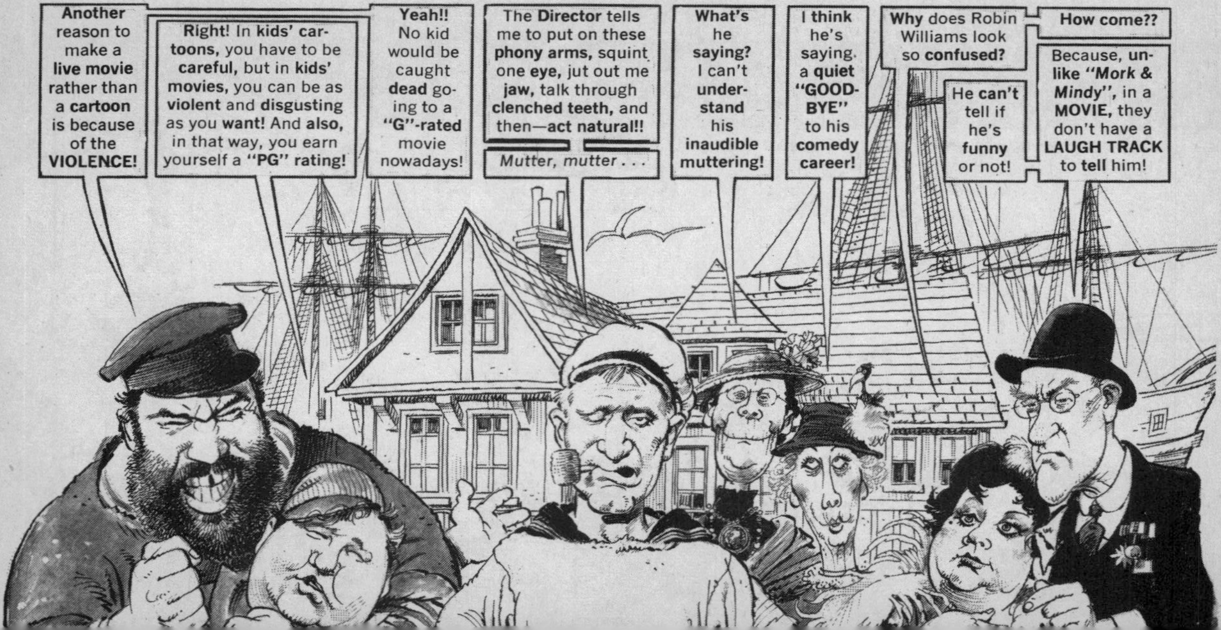

Another reason to make a live movie rather than a cartoon is because of the VIOLENCE!
Right! In kids' cartoons, you have to be careful, but in kids' movies, you can be as violent and disgusting as you want! And also, in that way, you earn yourself a "PG" rating!
Yeah!! No kid would be caught dead going to a "G"-rated movie nowadays!
The Director tells me to put on these phony arms, squint one eye, jut out me jaw, talk through clenched teeth, and then—act natural!!
Mutter, mutter . . .
What's he saying? I can't understand his inaudible muttering!
I think he's saying. a quiet "GOOD-BYE" to his comedy career!
Why does Robin Williams look so confused?
He can't tell if he's funny or not!
How come??
Because, unlike "Mork & Mindy", in a MOVIE, they don't have a LAUGH TRACK to tell him!

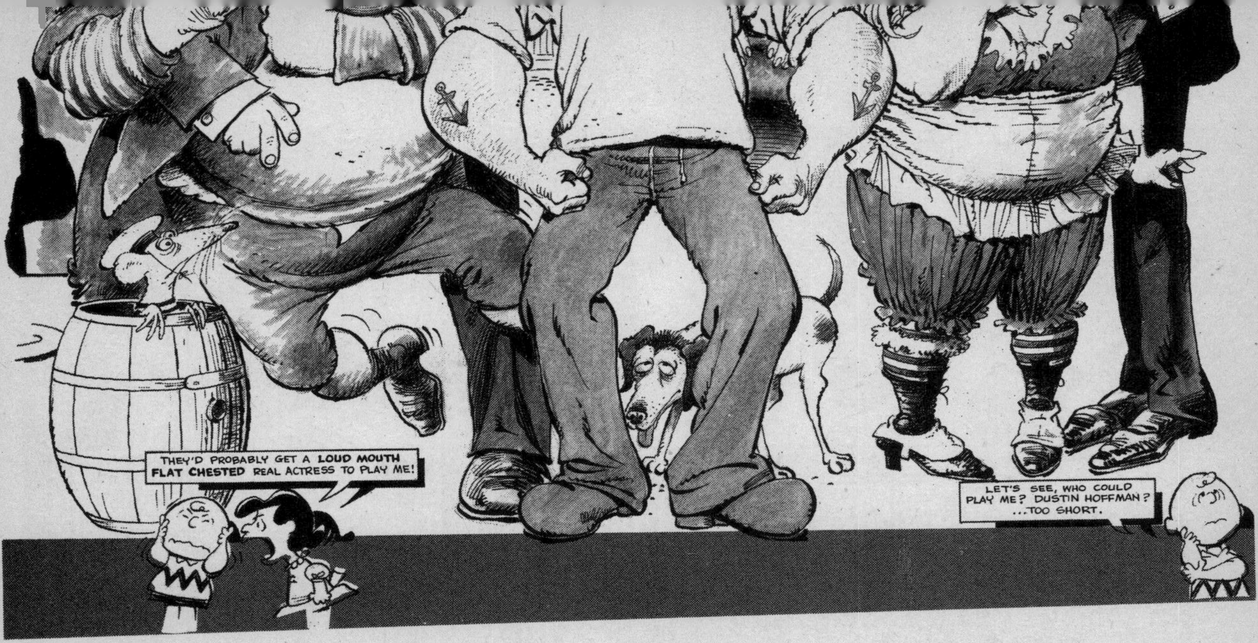
THEY'D PROBABLY GET A LOUD MOUTH FLAT CHESTED REAL ACTRESS TO PLAY ME!
LET'S SEE, WHO COULD PLAY ME? DUSTIN HOFFMAN? ...TOO SHORT.

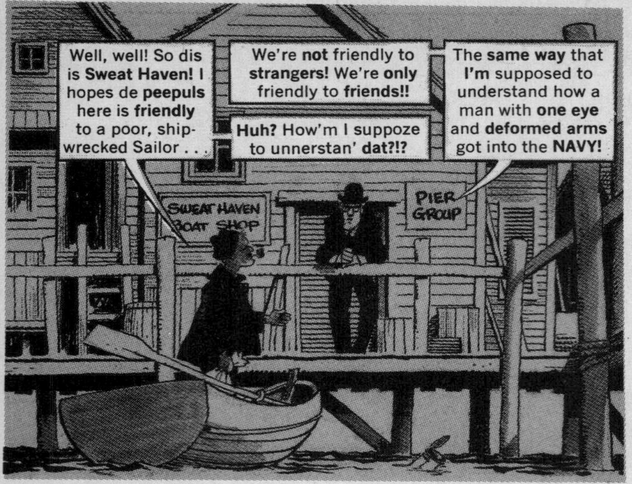
Well, well! So dis is Sweat Haven! I hopes de peepuls here is friendly to a poor, ship-wrecked Sailor . . .
We're not friendly to strangers! We're only friendly to friends!!
Huh? How'm I suppoze to unnerstan' dat?!?
The same way that I'm supposed to understand how a man with one eye and deformed arms got into the NAVY!
SWEAT HAVEN BOAT SHOP
PIER GROUP

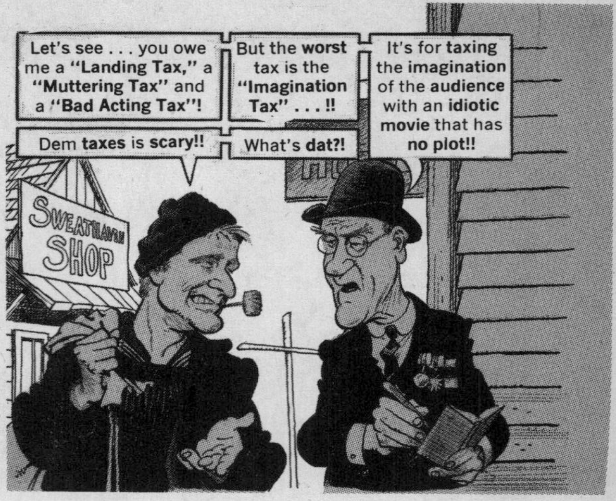
Let's see . . . you owe me a "Landing Tax," a "Muttering Tax" and a "Bad Acting Tax"!
Dem taxes is scary!!
But the worst tax is the "Imagination Tax" . . . !!
What's dat?!
It's for taxing the imagination of the audience with an idiotic movie that has no plot!!
SWEATHAVEN SHOP

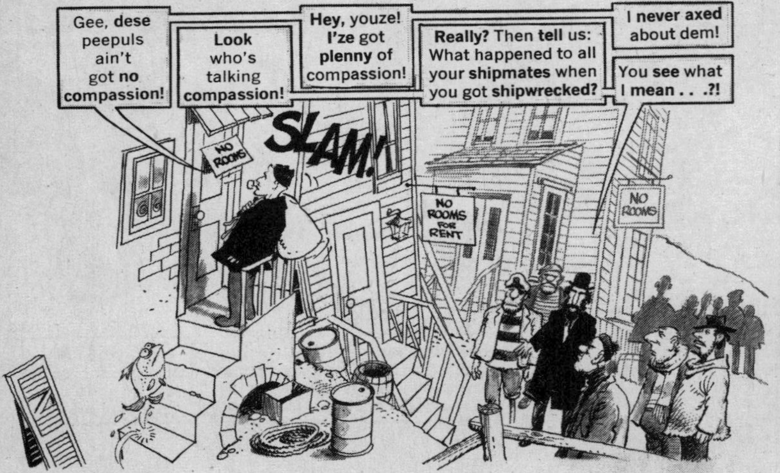
Gee, **dese** peepuls ain't got **no compassion!**
Look who's talking **compassion!**
Hey, youze! **I'ze** got **plenny** of compassion!
Really? Then **tell** us: What happened to all your **shipmates** when you got **shipwrecked?**
I **never axed** about dem!
You **see** what I **mean . . .?!**
SLAM!
NO ROOMS
NO ROOMS FOR RENT
NO ROOMS

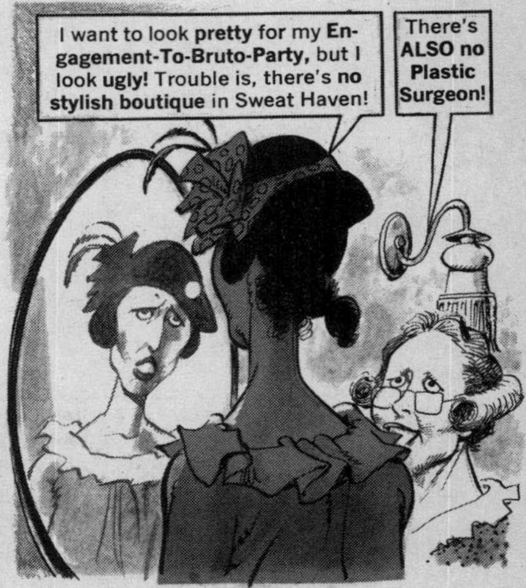
I want to look **pretty** for my **Engagement-To-Bruto-Party,** but I look **ugly!** Trouble is, there's **no stylish boutique** in Sweat Haven!
There's **ALSO no Plastic Surgeon!**

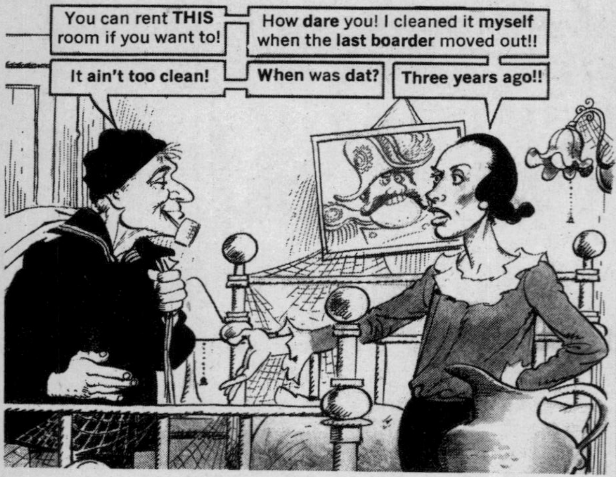
You can rent **THIS** room if you want to!
How **dare** you! I cleaned it **myself** when the **last boarder** moved out!!
It **ain't too clean!**
When was **dat?**
Three years ago!!

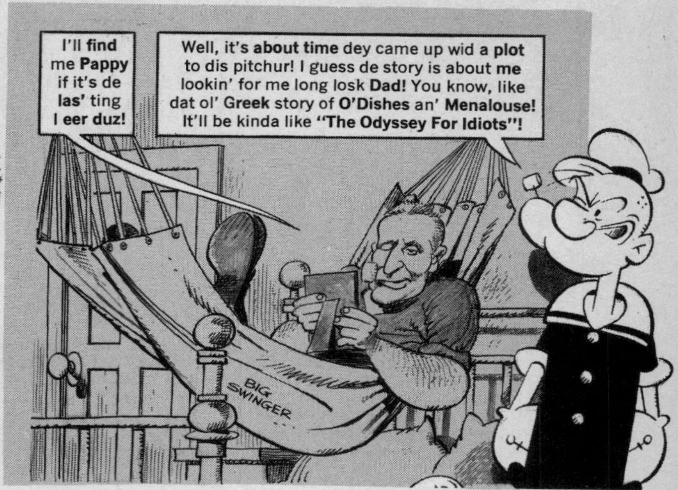
I'll **find** me **Pappy** if it's de **las'** ting **I eer duz!**
Well, it's **about time** dey came up wid a **plot** to dis pitchur! I guess de story is about **me** lookin' for me long losk **Dad!** You know, like dat ol' **Greek** story of **O'Dishes** an' **Menalouse!** It'll be kinda like **"The Odyssey For Idiots"!**
BIG SWINGER

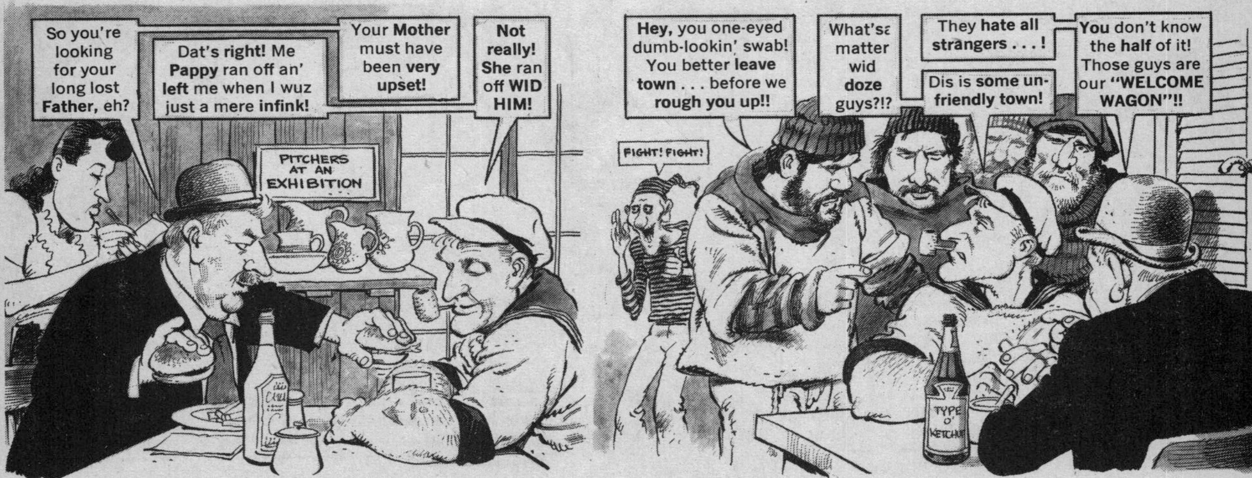
So you're looking for your long lost **Father**, eh?
Dat's **right!** Me **Pappy** ran off an' **left** me when I wuz just a mere **infink!**
Your **Mother** must have been **very upset!**
Not really! She ran off **WID HIM!**
PITCHERS AT AN EXHIBITION
FIGHT! FIGHT!
Hey, you one-eyed dumb-lookin' swab! You better **leave town** . . . before we **rough you up!!**
What'sa matter wid **doze** guys?!?
They **hate all strangers . . . !**
Dis is **some un-friendly town!**
You don't know the **half** of it! Those guys are our **"WELCOME WAGON"!!**
TYPE O' KETCHUP

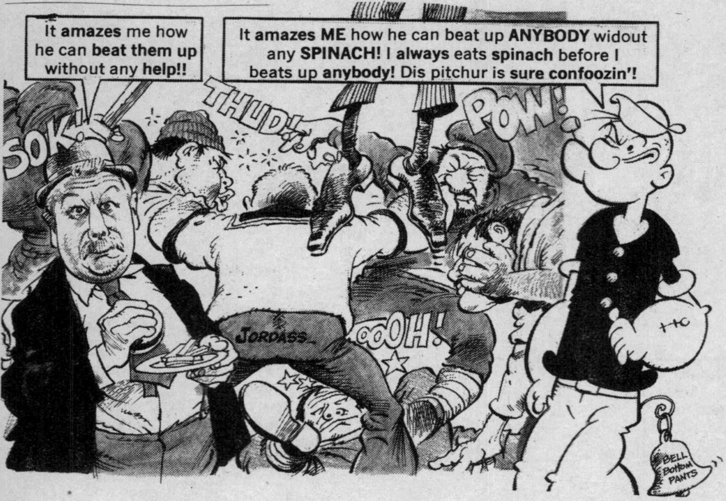
SOK!
It amazes me how he can beat them up without any help!!
THUD!
It amazes ME how he can beat up ANYBODY widout any SPINACH! I always eats spinach before I beats up anybody! Dis pitchur is sure confoozin'!
POW!
OOOH!
JORDASS
BELL BOTTOM PANTS
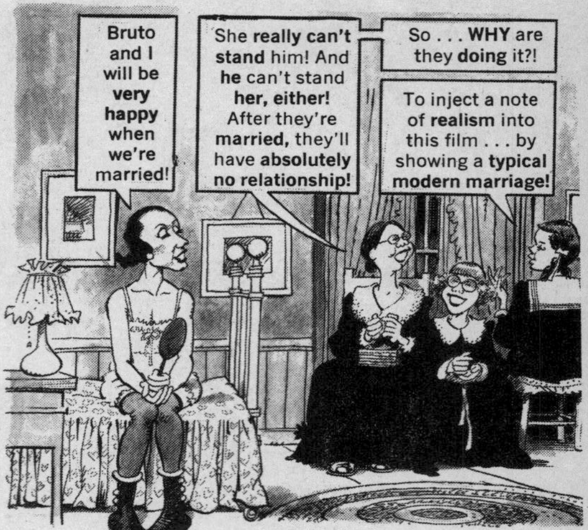
Bruto and I will be very happy when we're married!
She really can't stand him! And he can't stand her, either! After they're married, they'll have absolutely no relationship!
So . . . WHY are they doing it?!
To inject a note of realism into this film . . . by showing a typical modern marriage!

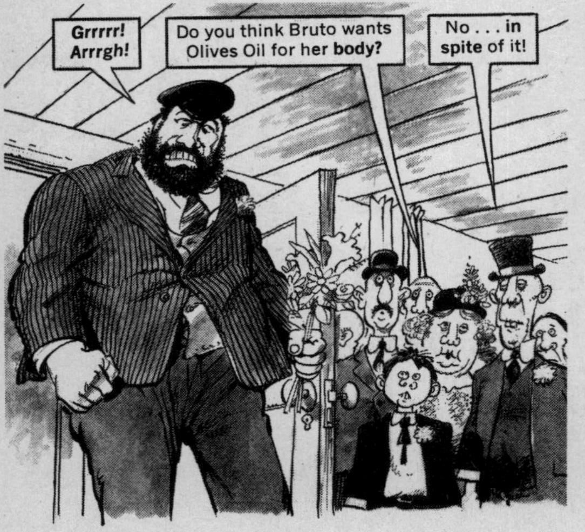
Grrrrr! Arrrgh!
Do you think Bruto wants Olives Oil for her body?
No . . . in spite of it!

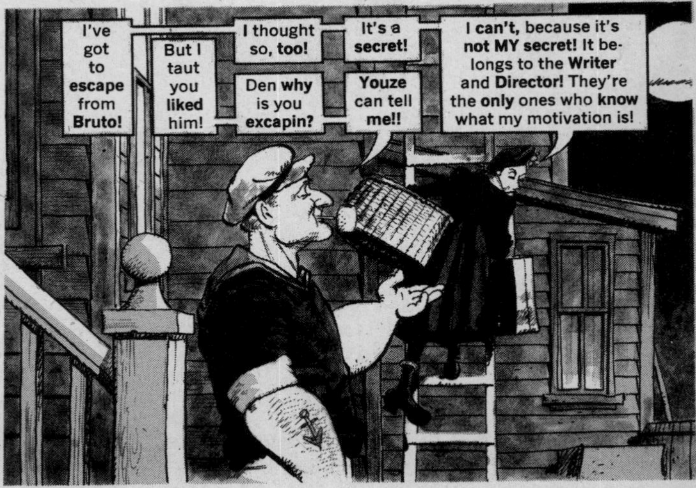
I've got to escape from Bruto!
But I taut you liked him!
I thought so, too!
Den why is you excapin?
It's a secret!
Youze can tell me!!
I can't, because it's not MY secret! It belongs to the Writer and Director! They're the only ones who know what my motivation is!

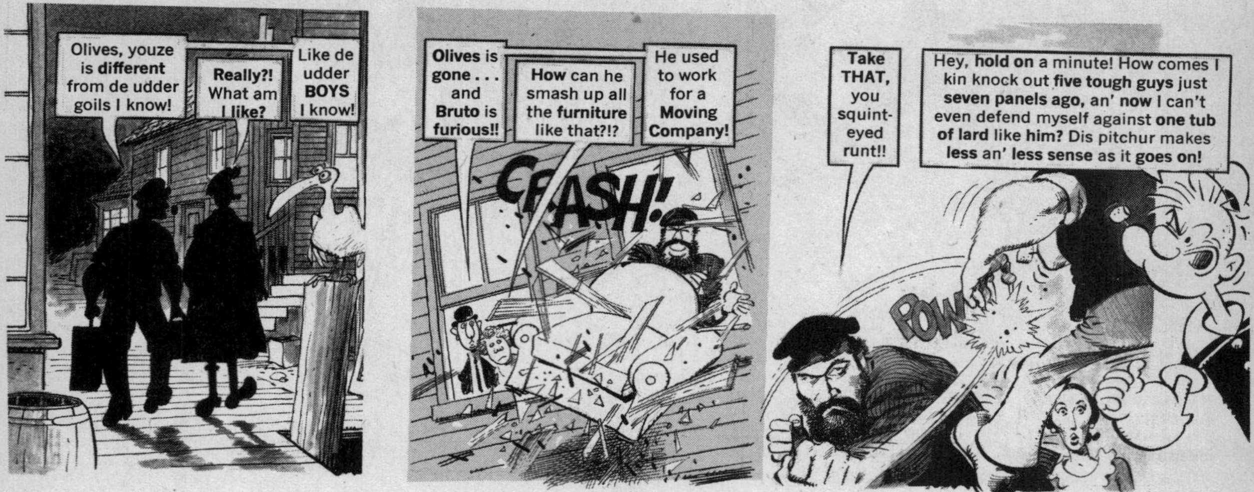

Olives, youze is **different** from de udder goils I know!
Really?! What am **I like?**
Like de udder **BOYS** I know!
Olives is **gone . . .** and **Bruto** is **furious!!**
How can he smash up all the **furniture** like that?!?
He used to work for a **Moving Company!**
CRASH!
Take THAT, you squint-eyed runt!!
Hey, **hold on** a minute! How comes I kin knock out **five tough guys** just **seven panels ago,** an' **now** I can't even defend myself against **one tub of lard** like **him?** Dis pitchur makes **less** an' **less sense** as it **goes on!**
POW

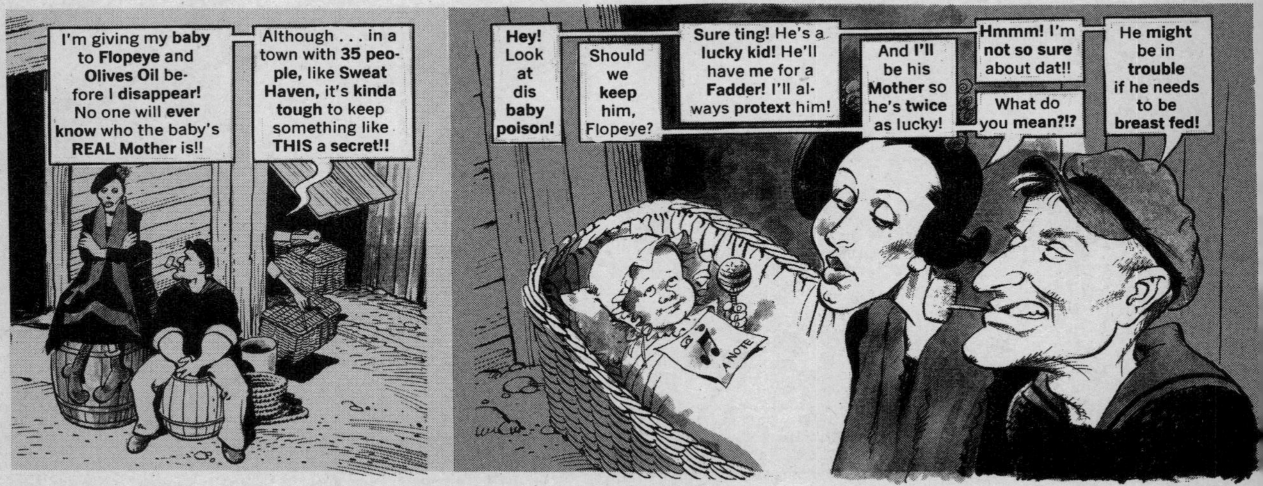
I'm giving my baby to Flopeye and Olives Oil before I disappear! No one will ever know who the baby's REAL Mother is!!
Although . . . in a town with 35 people, like Sweat Haven, it's kinda tough to keep something like THIS a secret!!
Hey! Look at dis baby poison!
Should we keep him, Flopeye?
Sure ting! He's a lucky kid! He'll have me for a Fadder! I'll always protext him!
And I'll be his Mother so he's twice as lucky!
Hmmm! I'm not so sure about dat!!
What do you mean?!?
He might be in trouble if he needs to be breast fed!
A NOTE

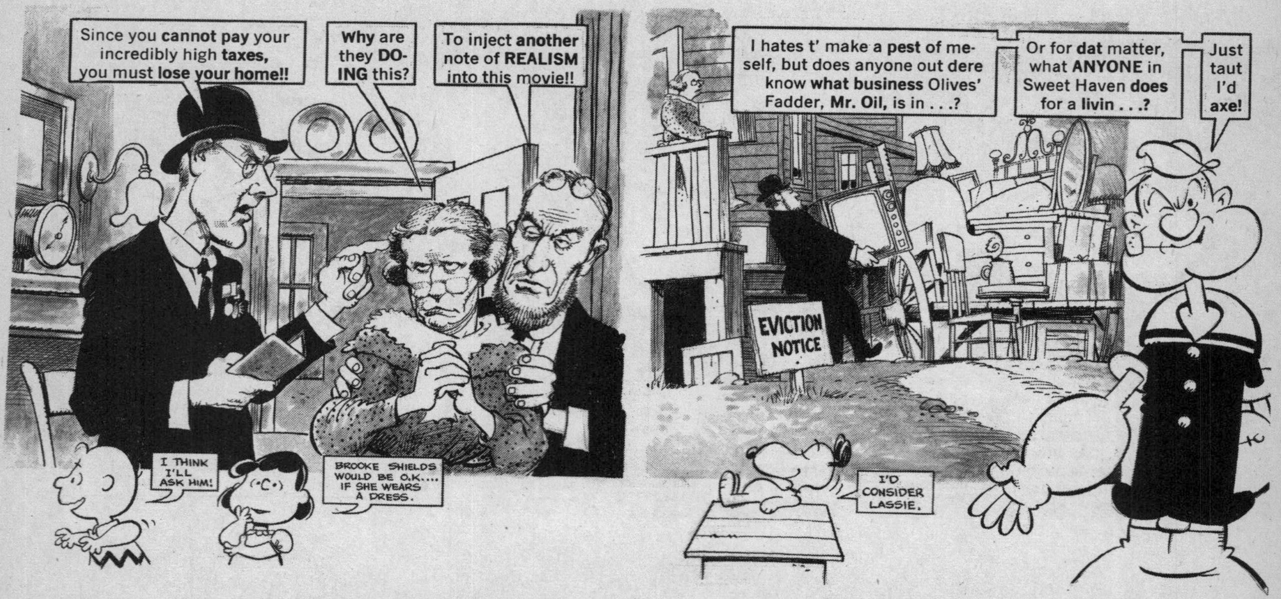
Since you cannot pay your incredibly high taxes, you must lose your home!!
Why are they DOING this?
To inject another note of REALISM into this movie!!
I THINK I'LL ASK HIM!
BROOKE SHIELDS WOULD BE O.K.... IF SHE WEARS A DRESS.
I hates t' make a pest of meself, but does anyone out dere know what business Olives' Fadder, Mr. Oil, is in . . .?
Or for dat matter, what ANYONE in Sweet Haven does for a livin . . .?
Just taut I'd axe!
EVICTION NOTICE
I'D CONSIDER LASSIE.

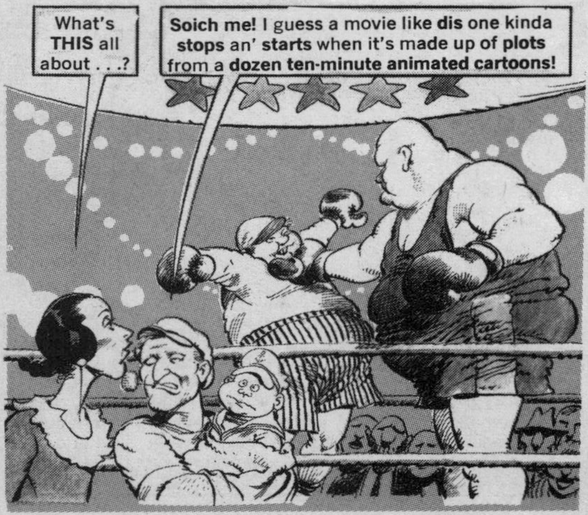
What's **THIS** all about . . .?
Soich me! I guess a movie like **dis** one kinda **stops** an' **starts** when it's made up of **plots** from a **dozen ten-minute animated cartoons!**

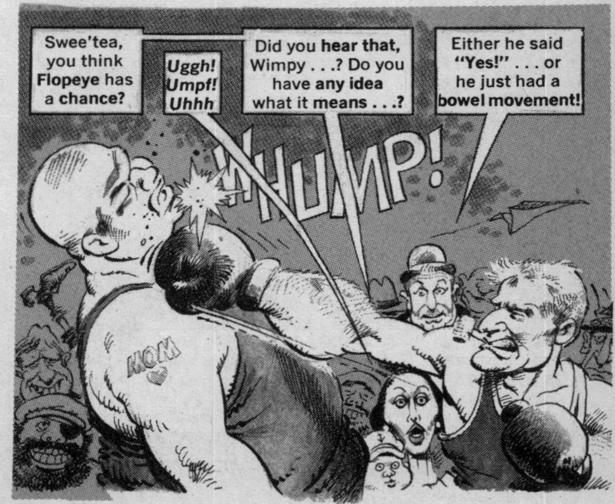
Swee'tea, you think **Flopeye** has a **chance?**
Uggh! Umpf! Uhhh
WHUMP!
Did you **hear that,** Wimpy . . .? Do you have **any idea** what it **means . . .?**
Either he said **"Yes!"** . . . or he just had a **bowel movement!**
MOM

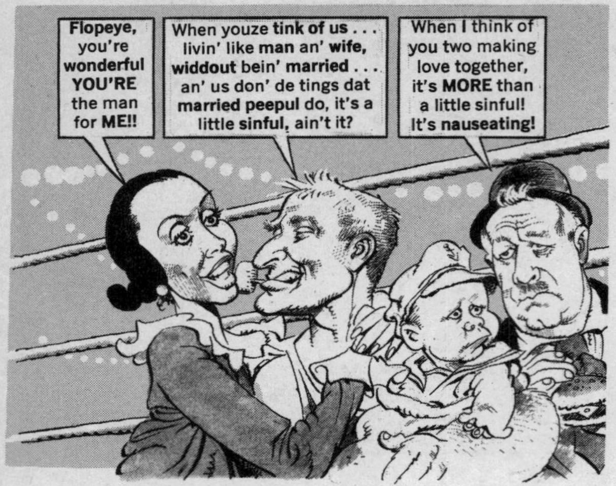
Flopeye, you're wonderful YOU'RE the man for ME!!
When youze tink of us . . . livin' like man an' wife, widdout bein' married . . . an' us don' de tings dat married peepul do, it's a little sinful, ain't it?
When I think of you two making love together, it's MORE than a little sinful! It's nauseating!

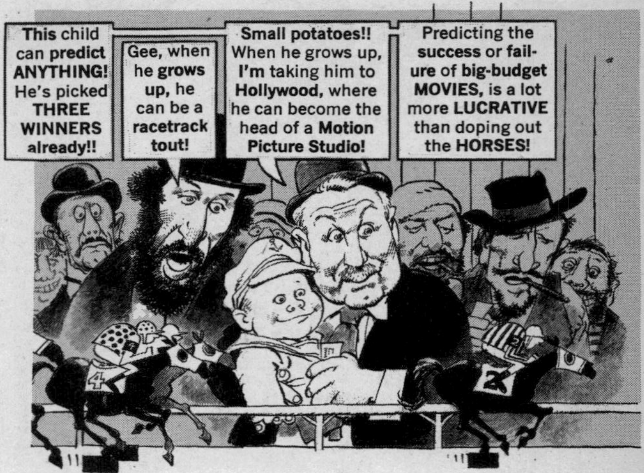
This child can predict ANYTHING! He's picked THREE WINNERS already!!
Gee, when he grows up, he can be a racetrack tout!
Small potatoes!! When he grows up, I'm taking him to Hollywood, where he can become the head of a Motion Picture Studio!
Predicting the success or failure of big-budget MOVIES, is a lot more LUCRATIVE than doping out the HORSES!

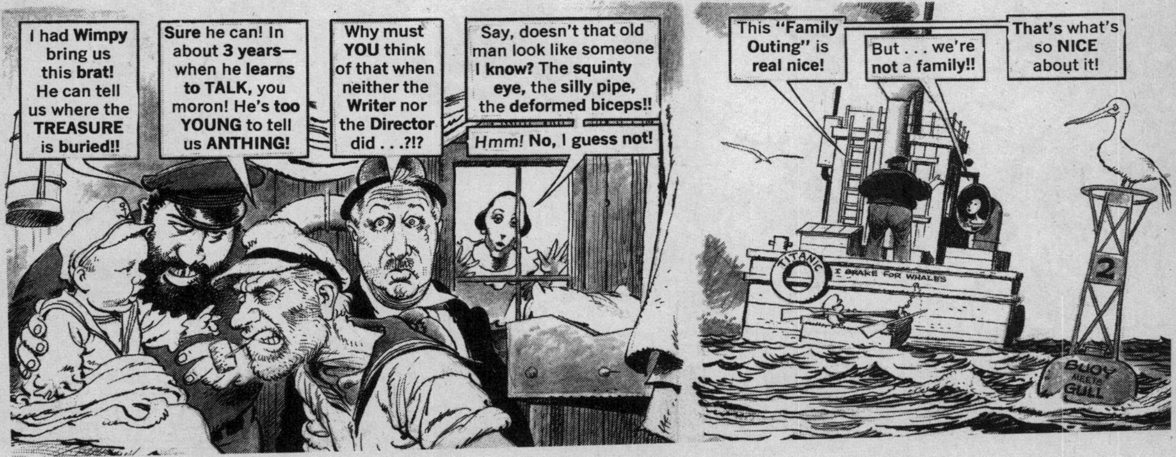
I had Wimpy bring us this brat! He can tell us where the TREASURE is buried!!
Sure he can! In about 3 years—when he learns to TALK, you moron! He's too YOUNG to tell us ANTHING!
Why must YOU think of that when neither the Writer nor the Director did . . .?!?
Say, doesn't that old man look like someone I know? The squinty eye, the silly pipe, the deformed biceps!!
Hmm! No, I guess not!
This "Family Outing" is real nice!
But . . . we're not a family!!
That's what's so NICE about it!
TITANIC
I BRAKE FOR WHALES
2
BUOY MEETS GULL

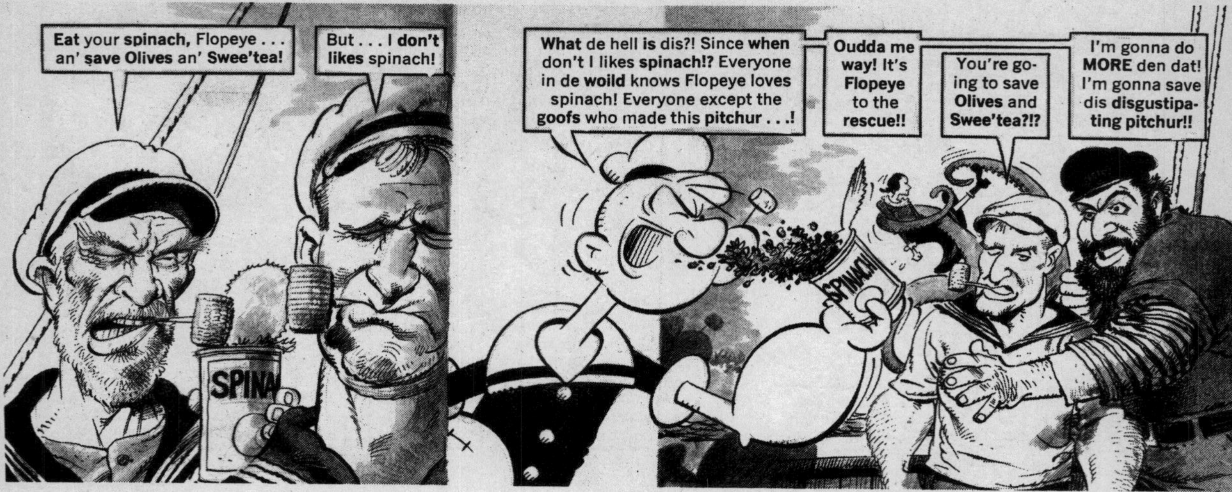

Eat your spinach, Flopeye . . . an' save Olives an' Swee'tea!
But . . . I don't likes spinach!
What de hell is dis?! Since when don't I likes spinach!? Everyone in de woild knows Flopeye loves spinach! Everyone except the goofs who made this pitchur . . .!
Oudda me way! It's Flopeye to the rescue!!
You're going to save Olives and Swee'tea?!?
I'm gonna do MORE den dat! I'm gonna save dis disgustipating pitchur!!
SPINA
SPINACH

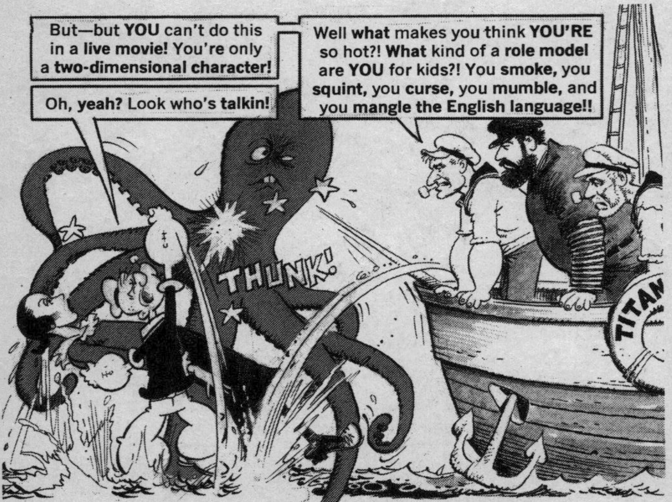
But—but YOU can't do this in a live movie! You're only a two-dimensional character!
Oh, yeah? Look who's talkin!
Well what makes you think YOU'RE so hot?! What kind of a role model are YOU for kids?! You smoke, you squint, you curse, you mumble, and you mangle the English language!!
THUNK!

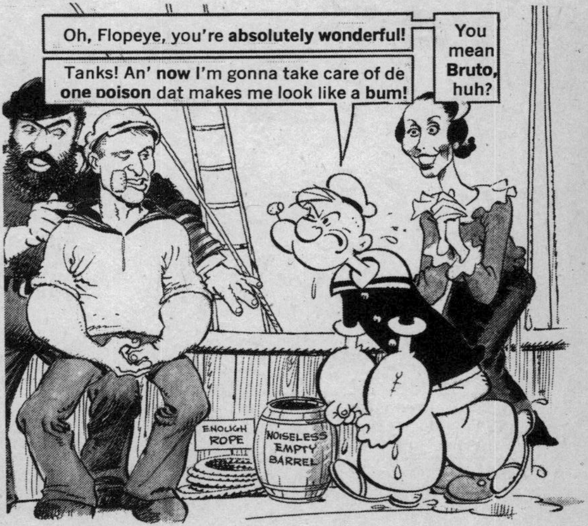
Oh, Flopeye, you're absolutely wonderful!
Tanks! An' now I'm gonna take care of de one poison dat makes me look like a bum!
You mean Bruto, huh?
ENOUGH ROPE
NOISELESS EMPTY BARREL

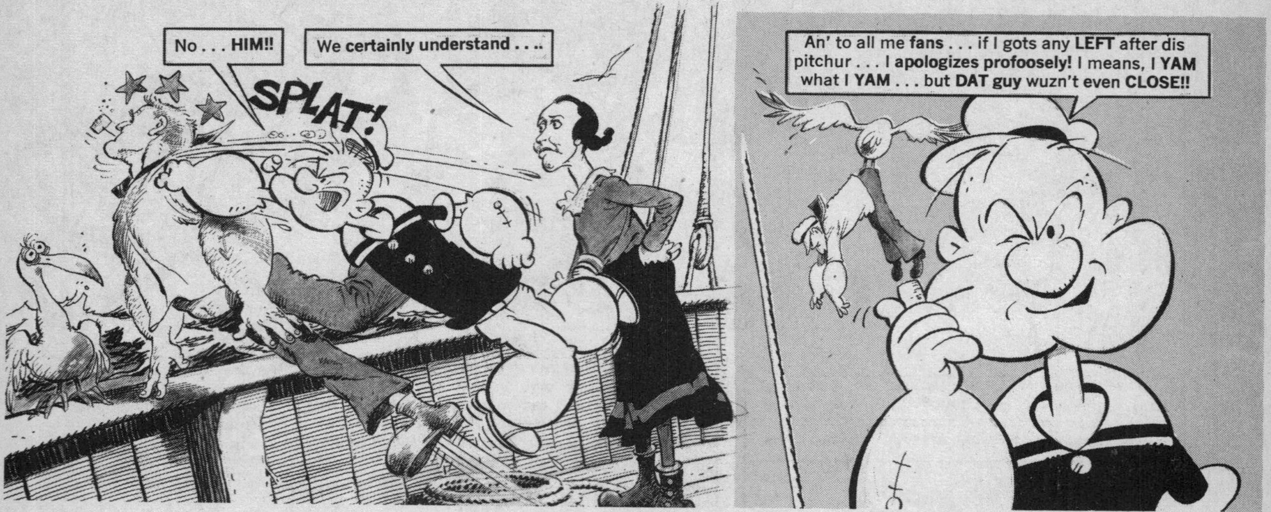
No . . . HIM!!
We certainly understand . . ..
SPLAT!
An' to all me fans . . . if I gots any LEFT after dis pitchur . . . I apologizes profoosely! I means, I YAM what I YAM . . . but DAT guy wuzn't even CLOSE!!

SAILOR MAN-SLAUGHTER DEPT.

DON MARTIN LOOKS AT POPEYE

This guy's one for the **books,** Sir! He's **out of uniform,** and he's been **AWOL for forty years!!**

AIRPORT SECURITY
DING DING DING DING DING DING DING DING
Okay, Mac! What have you got stashed in your shirt?
One false move and I blow your head off!!
DING DING DING DING DING DING DING DING DING DING DING
SPINACH
KLUNK

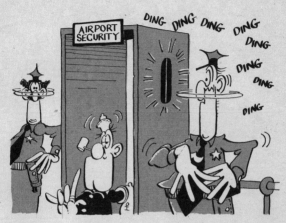

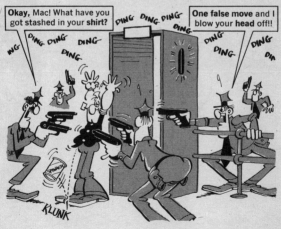

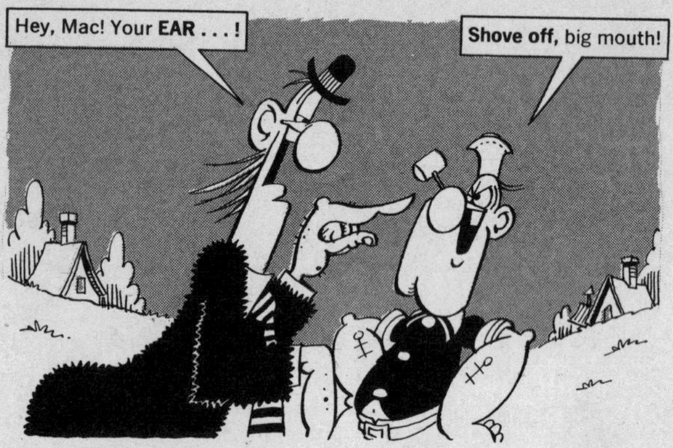
Hey, Mac! Your **EAR . . .!**
Shove off, big mouth!

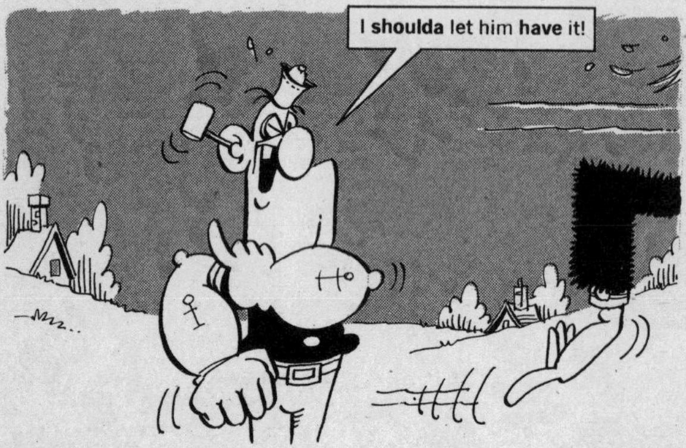
I **shoulda** let him **have** it!

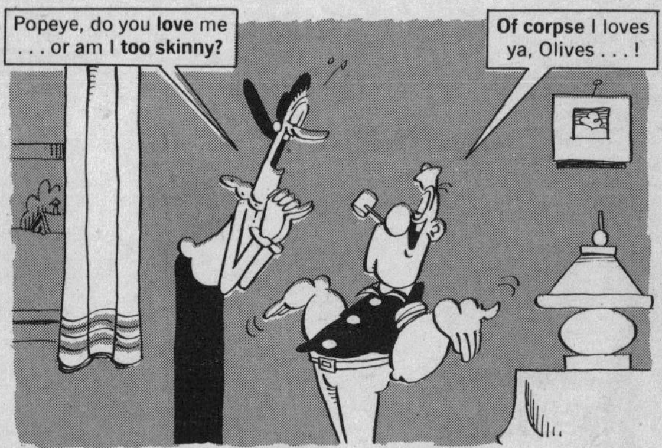

Popeye, do you **love** me . . . or am I **too skinny?**
Of corpse I loves ya, Olives . . . !

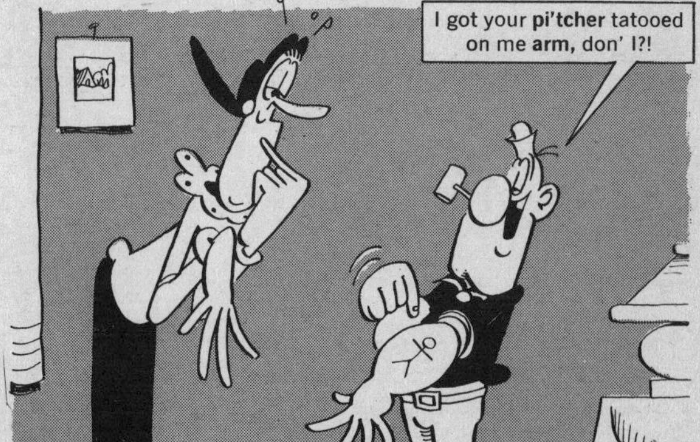

I got your **pi'tcher** tatooed on me **arm,** don' I?!

Popeye, you grow your own spinach! Tell me, how can common spinach give you so much strength?
SPINACH
WARNING
FALL OUT
AREA
Beats me . . . !

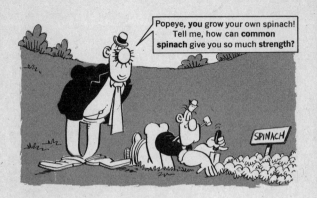

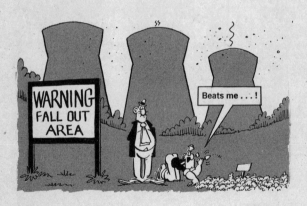

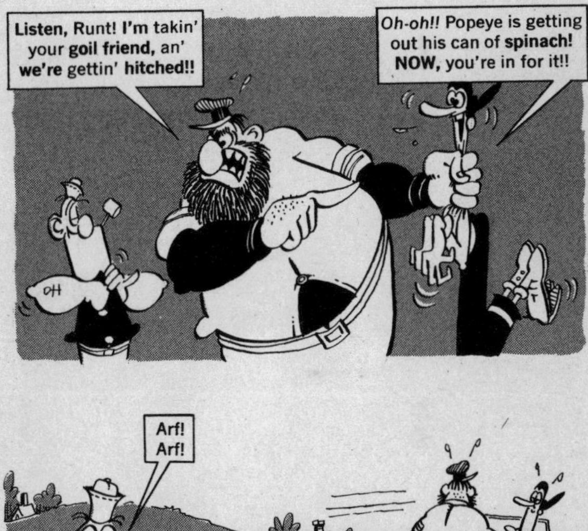
Listen, Runt! **I'm** takin' your **goil friend,** an' **we're** gettin' **hitched!!**
Oh-oh!! Popeye is getting out his can of **spinach! NOW,** you're in for it!!

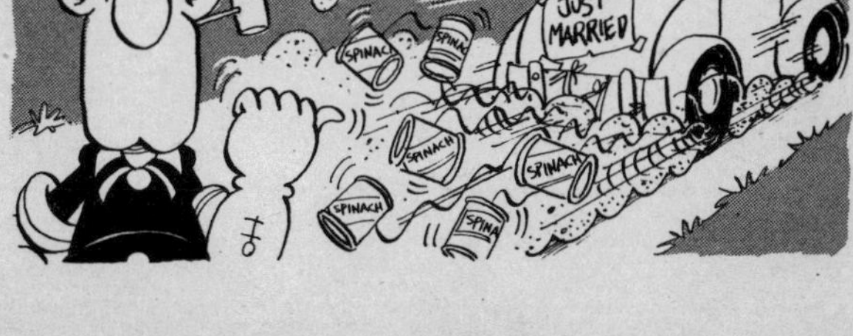
Arf! Arf!
JUST MARRIED
SPINACH

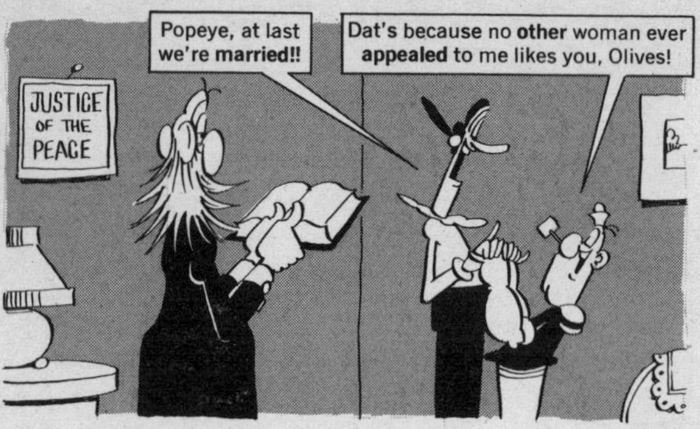
Popeye, at last we're married!!
Dat's because no other woman ever appealed to me likes you, Olives!
JUSTICE OF THE PEACE

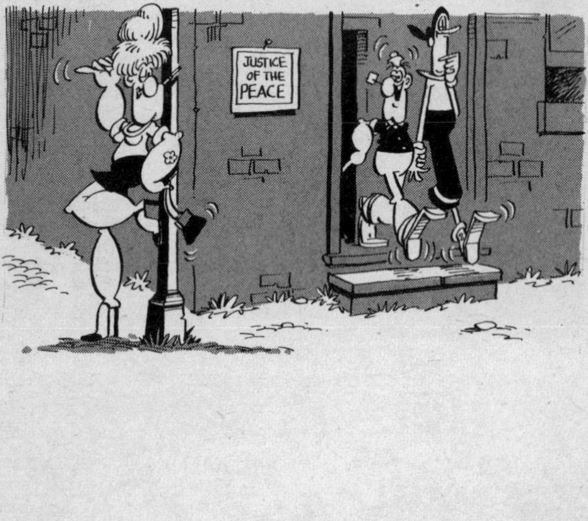
JUSTICE OF THE PEACE

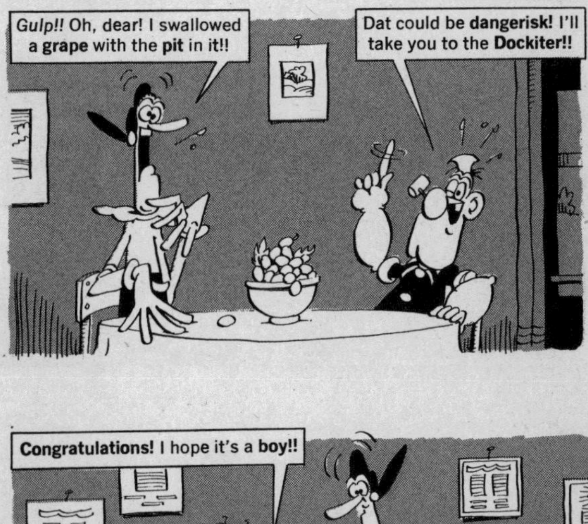

Gulp!! Oh, dear! I swallowed a **grape** with the **pit** in it!!
Dat could be **dangerisk!** I'll take you to the **Dockiter!!**

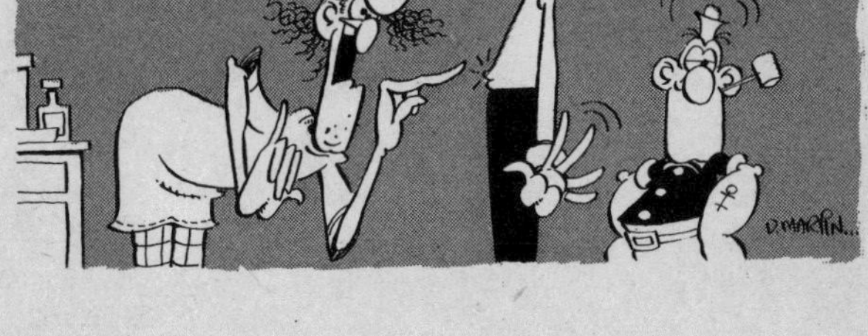

Congratulations! I hope it's a **boy!!**
D.MARTIN...

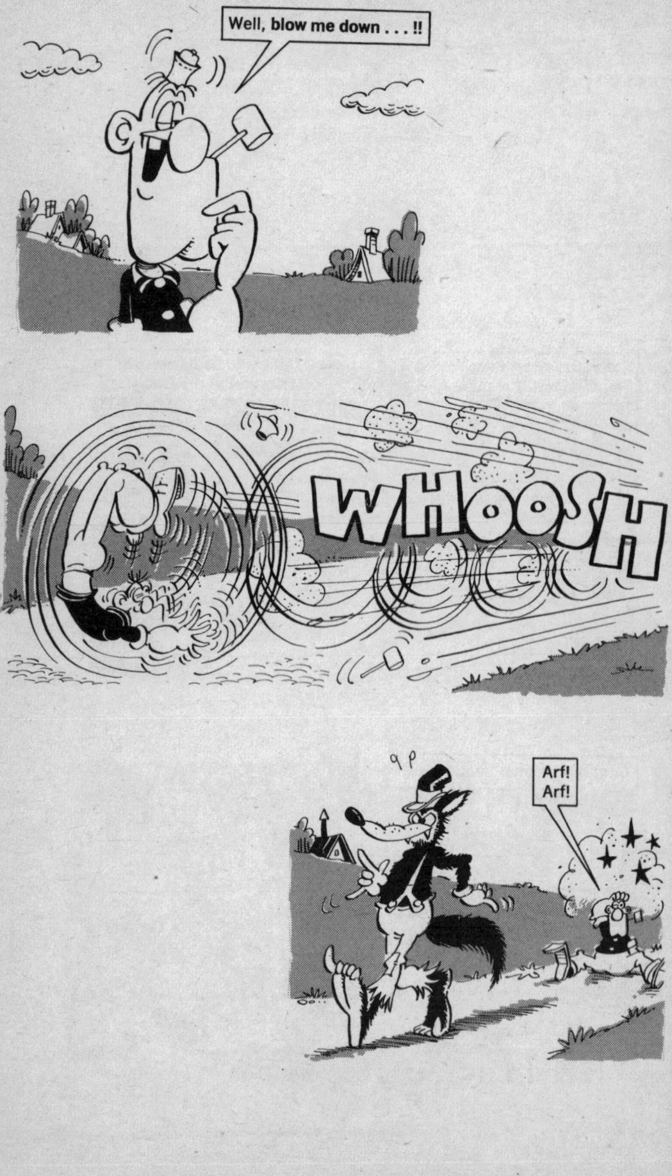
Well, blow me down . . . !!
WHOOSH
Arf!
Arf!

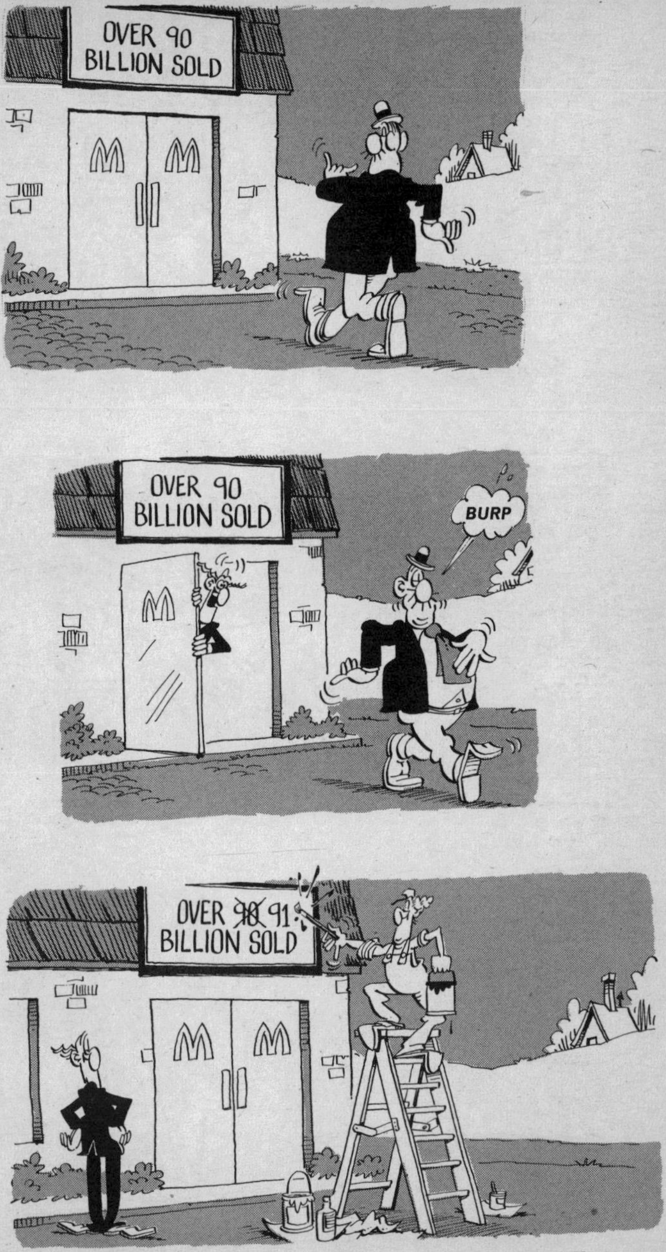
OVER 90 BILLION SOLD
OVER 90 BILLION SOLD
BURP
OVER ~~90~~ 91 BILLION SOLD

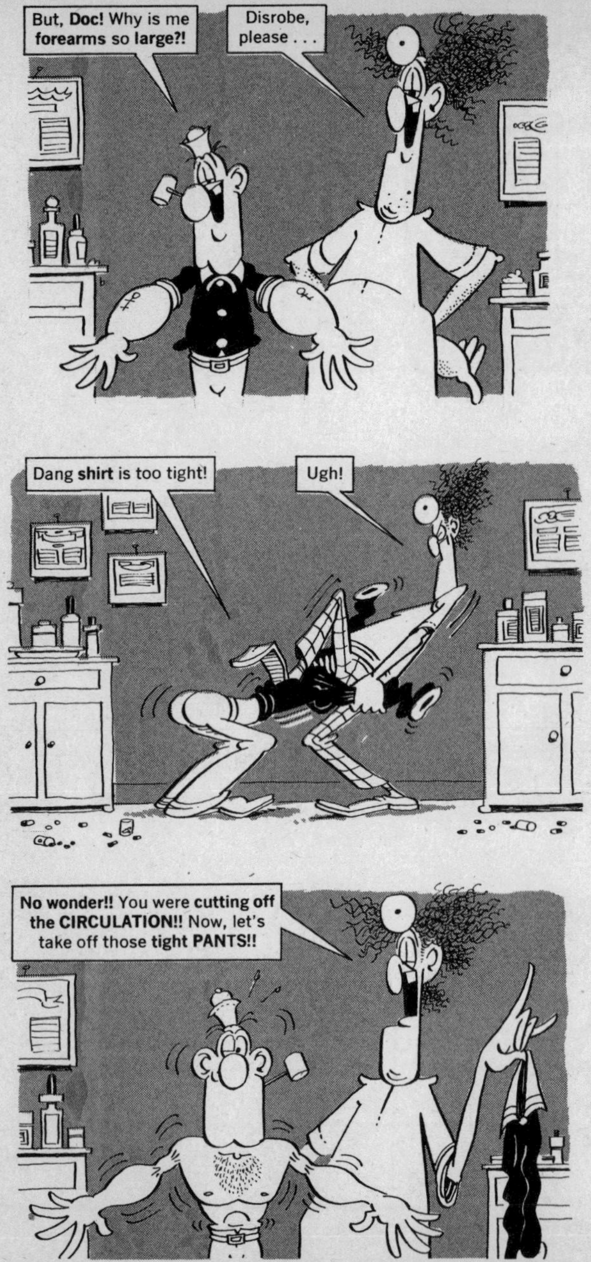
But, Doc! Why is me forearms so large?!
Disrobe, please . . .
Dang shirt is too tight!
Ugh!
No wonder!! You were cutting off the CIRCULATION!! Now, let's take off those tight PANTS!!

With organ transplants becoming increasingly commonplace these days, many people now carry "Donor Cards" authorizing the use of their anatomical parts upon their deaths. But what about the famous (or infamous) people of the world, who might want certain "modifications" to their donations? MAD speculates on these "restrictions" with . . .

CUSTOMIZED

ORGAN

DONOR

CARDS

FOR SOME VERY SPECIAL DONORS

WRITER: DENNIS SNEE

U.C.L.A. MEDICAL CENTER
Organ Donor Card

JOHNNY CARSON

I hereby bequeath my usable organs to the UCLA Medical Center, unless...

I die on a Monday, in which case my "guest donor" will discharge these responsibilities; or...

I die on a Tuesday, when only my vital organs—or "The Best Of Carson"—shall be donated.

ORGAN DONOR CERTIFICATE

Richard Milhous Nixon

I wish to donate my ex-Presidential organs to medical science upon my death, providing that:

(1) They are utilized only by my fellow Americans. This does not include any members of the news media, or any registered Democrats.

(2) They are accepted without comment or speculation concerning the 18 inch gap in my lower intestinal tract, and

(3) My estate is not offered a sum less than one million dollars for their use on a network television "special" by David Frost.

Richard M. Nixon

HOLLYWOOD SQUARE MEDICAL CENTER
Organ Donor Certificate

RICH LITTLE

I hereby bequeath my body to medical science with the stipulation that the attending physician make absolutely certain that I am in fact deceased, and not merely impersonating a famous dead celebrity.

Rich Little

LOUISVILLE GENERAL HOSPITAL
Organ Donor Certificate

MUHAMMAD ALI

I donate all my organs
to worthy donees;
Just one thing I ask,
and that is to, please—

If I seem deceased,
let me set overnight;
'Cause I just may return
for one more 'final' fight!

ORGAN DONOR CARD
Cedars Of Lebanon Hospital

Don Rickles

Having made a fortune by insulting Blacks, Orientals, Chicanos, Tall People, Short People, Fat People, Skinny People, Bald People, Ugly People, Senior Citizens and other persons of every conceivable Race, Religion and National Origin, I hereby donate—upon my death—my organs to any member of the above-mentioned groups, with the exception of my tongue, which is considered a dangerous weapon and should be promptly destroyed.

THE ROONE ARLEDGE MEDICAL FACILITY AND TV SPORTS INFORMATION CENTER

Organ Donor Card
HOWARD COSELL

Yes, and what more natural a reaction that this: to give pause at such a momentous occasion when, by putting pen to paper and affixing one's signature, one is forever bound by a decision as irrevocable as it is eternal, to donate one's God-given anatomical gifts to the purpose of medical science. Of course, the idea is revolutionary! Of course, the idea is bold! And yet, I *do* intend, I *do* consent that my bodily organs be utilized by the scientific authorities in command at the moment I shed my mortal coil. Indeed, how noble, how right, how sportsman-like the notion that one's functionable remains survive one's brief encounter with this temporal sphere. Certainly, it is not my intent nor purpose to wax melifluous at this juncture, and yet I

(Continued on the other side)

UGANDA STATE HOSPITAL

ORGAN DONOR CERTIFICATE

This is to certify that His Excellency President Field Marshal General Doctor Tenured Professor Licensed Electrician and Supreme Astronaut

IDI AMIN DADA

has decreed that upon his death, his bodily organs may be used by medical science as needed (as may the organs of any other persons found inside my digestive system) in the name of general progress and scientific advancement.

ORGAN DONOR FORM

The Amazing Kreskin

Knowing as I do not only the date, but also the circumstances that will surround my demise, I hereby give my blessings to the medical agencies that will send my liver to the Mayo Clinic, my kidneys to the Downstate Hospital, and my eyes to the New York Eye Bank. And to Walter Winkle of Bayonne, New Jersey, who will discover my dead body, I forgive you, Walter, for taking the cash from my wallet prior to reading this Donor Card.

T. A. Kreskin

MILLIONAIRE'S HOSPITAL OF BEVERLY HILLS

Organ Donor Release
NORMAN LEAR

In accordance with the philosophy I've utilized successfully as a television producer, I hereby decree that, upon my death, my usable organs be "spun-off" and featured individually in any new recipient's format deemed worthy and promising.

Norman Lear

ORGAN DONOR CARD
RALPH NADER

I hereby relinquish my body & bodily organs upon my death* for the purposes of medical science.

*Assuming I'm not burned beyond recognition in an automobile accident, or lost at sea in an airline disaster, or contaminated by radioactive waste material from a breeder reactor mishap, or abducted and mysteriously disposed of by persons whose livelihoods have been disrupted as a result of my various investigations, findings and statements.

UNIVERSITY OF GEORGIA MEDICAL CENTER
in association with
THE BREWMASTERS OF AMERICA
hereby ascribe their endorsement to the following donor information regarding

Billy Carter
First Brother, U.S. of A.

FIRST

That his vital organs may be flammable.

SECOND

That organs related to his digestive tract may be worn beyond any further use; and

THIRD

That the only organ which may have a useful lifespan is his brain, which, to the best of our knowledge, has not, so far, been taxed.

ORGAN DONOR INFORMATION
Robert "Evel" Knievel
DAREDEVIL ★ SHOWMAN ★ WAGER-MAKER

Having a minimum of original parts left, I would like to keep my remaining remains to myself!

Robert "Evel" Knievel

BERG'S-EYE VIEW DEPT.

THE LI
SIDE

DRUGS

Harry . . . I've got something **very serious** to tell you! I **discovered** that our **SON** is messing around with **DRUGS!**
Oh . . . ?!?
I **found** them in his **room!** He's been **on** them for months!
Hmmmm! This **IS** serious! Are you **SURE?** What **kind** is he using?

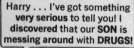

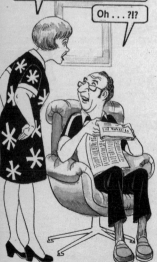

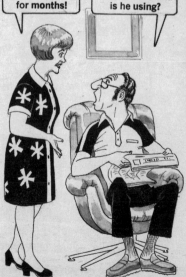

GHTER OF...

ARTIST & WRITER:
DAVE BERG

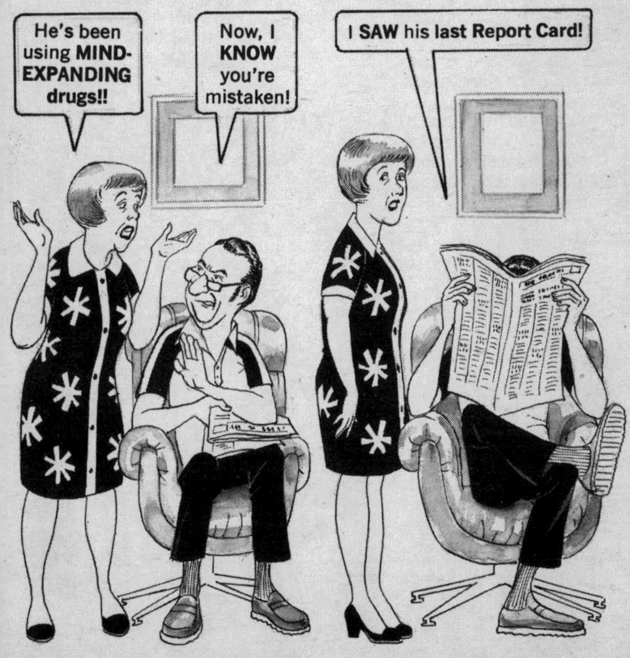
He's been using MIND-EXPANDING drugs!!
Now, I KNOW you're mistaken!
I SAW his last Report Card!

SOCIAL CALLS

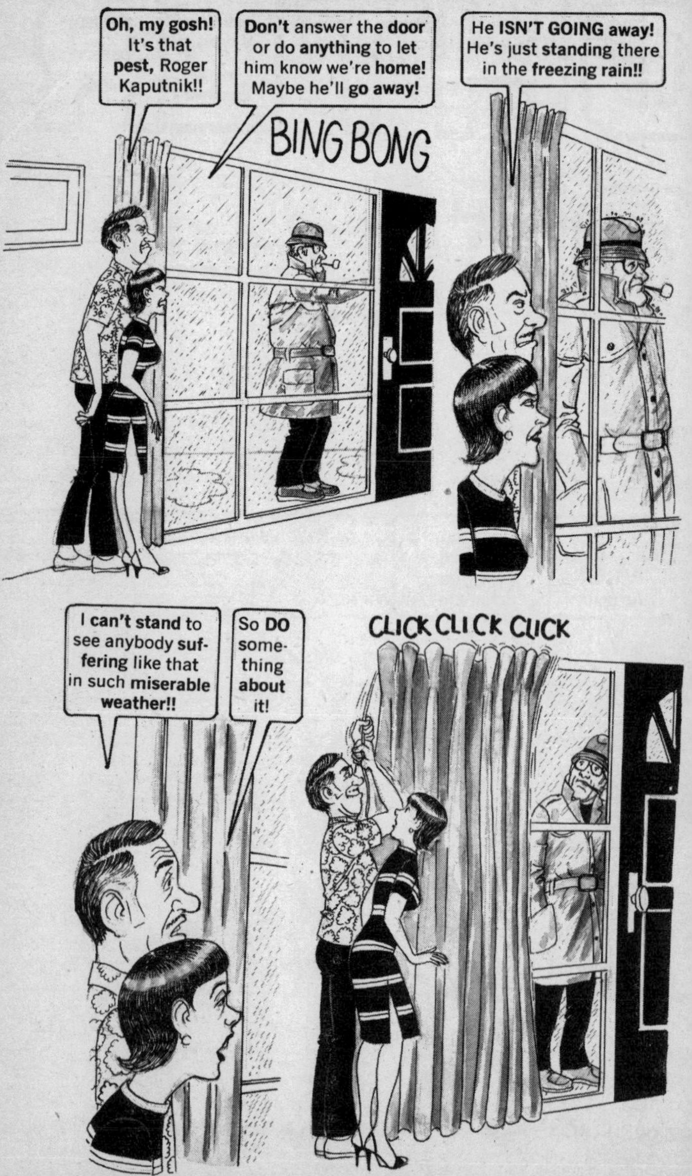

Oh, my gosh! It's that pest, Roger Kaputnik!!
Don't answer the door or do anything to let him know we're home! Maybe he'll go away!
BING BONG
He ISN'T GOING away! He's just standing there in the freezing rain!!
I can't stand to see anybody suf-fering like that in such miserable weather!!
So DO some-thing about it!
CLICK CLICK CLICK

CHILDPLAY

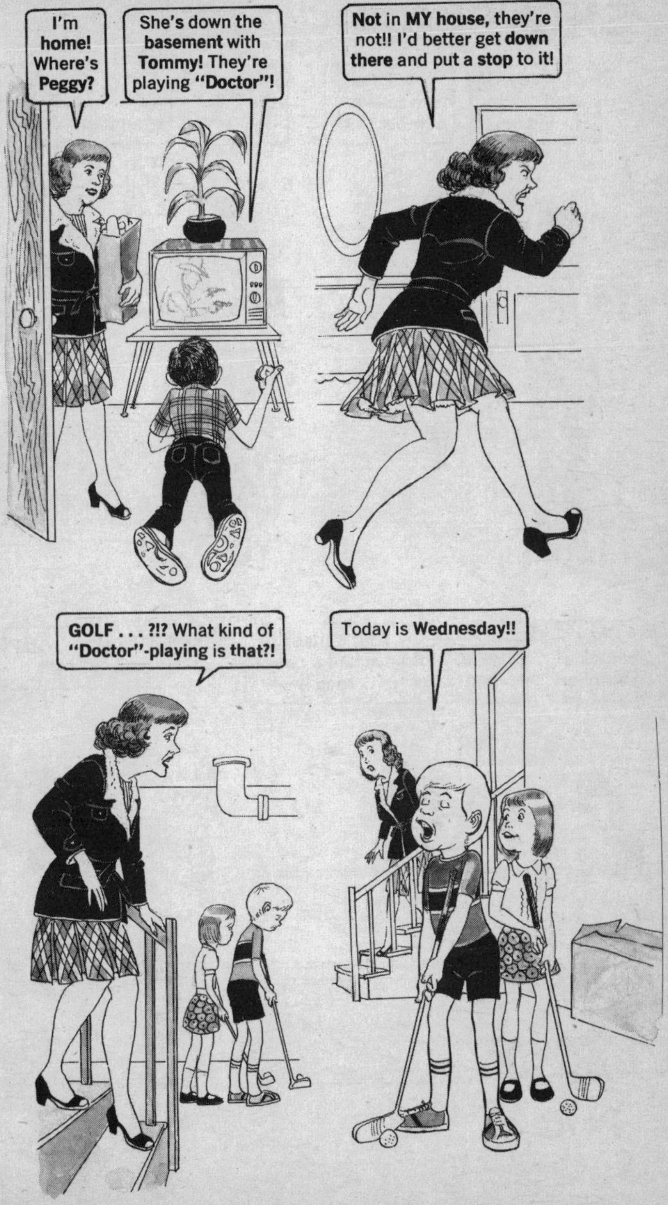
I'm home! Where's Peggy?
She's down the basement with Tommy! They're playing "Doctor"!
Not in MY house, they're not!! I'd better get down there and put a stop to it!
GOLF . . . ?!? What kind of "Doctor"-playing is that?!
Today is Wednesday!!

SHOPPING

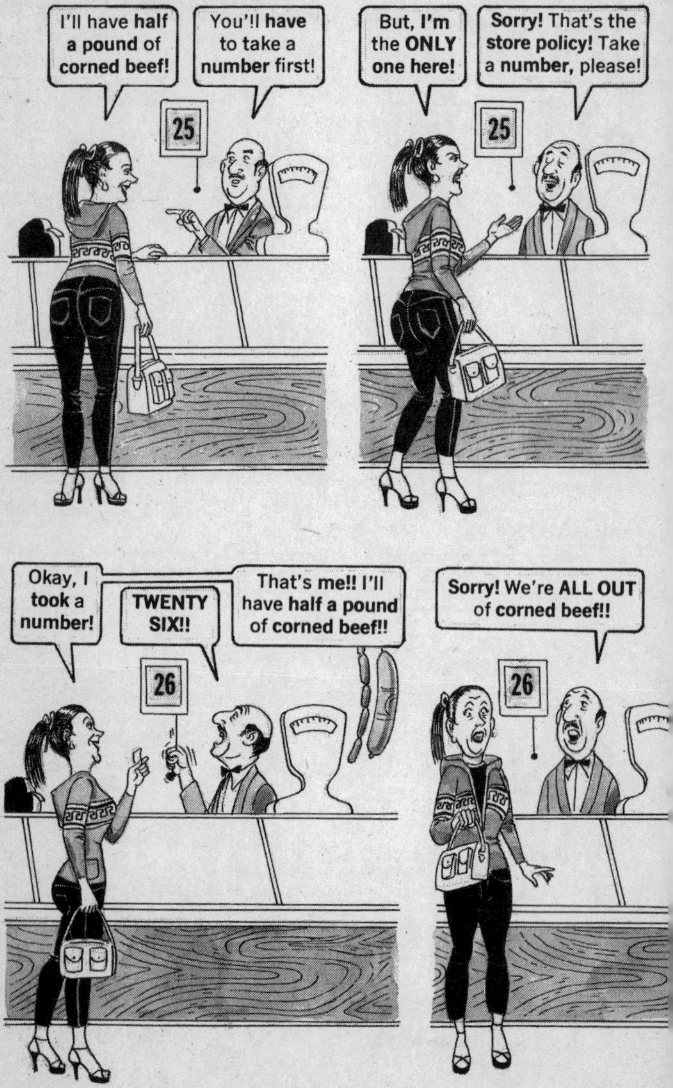

I'll have half a pound of corned beef!
You'll have to take a number first!
25
But, I'm the ONLY one here!
Sorry! That's the store policy! Take a number, please!
25
Okay, I took a number!
TWENTY SIX!!
That's me!! I'll have half a pound of corned beef!!
26
Sorry! We're ALL OUT of corned beef!!
26

GIFTS

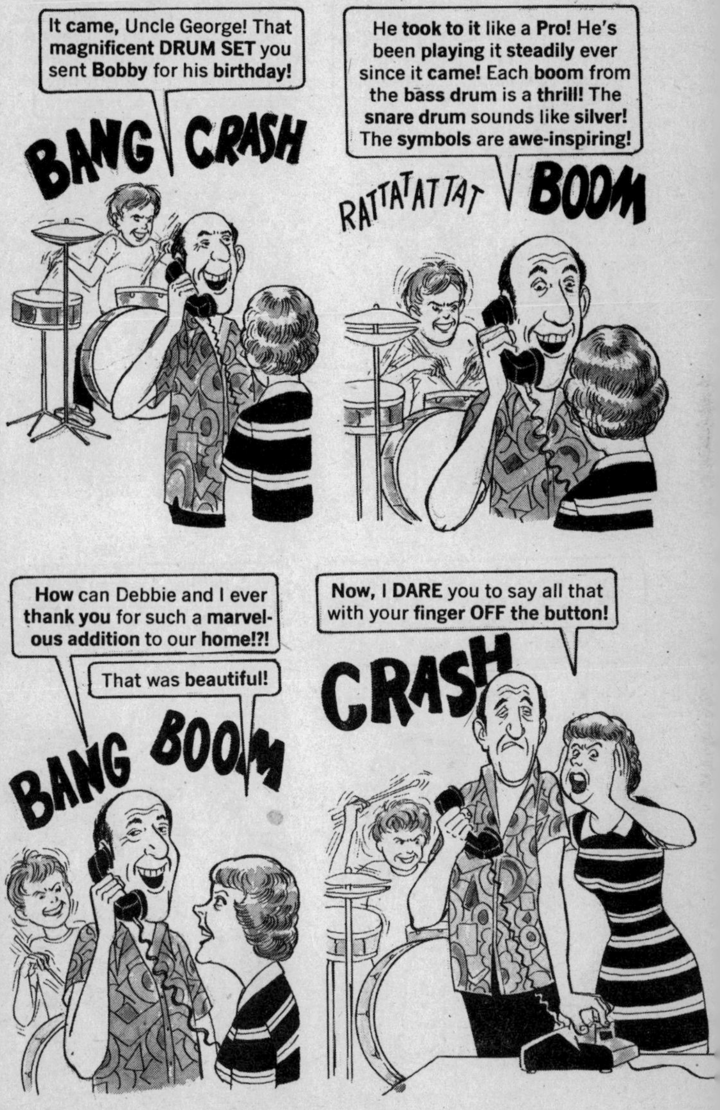
It came, Uncle George! That magnificent DRUM SET you sent Bobby for his birthday!
BANG
CRASH
He took to it like a Pro! He's been playing it steadily ever since it came! Each boom from the bass drum is a thrill! The snare drum sounds like silver! The symbols are awe-inspiring!
RATTATATTAT
BOOM
How can Debbie and I ever thank you for such a marvelous addition to our home!?!
That was beautiful!
BANG
BOOM
Now, I DARE you to say all that with your finger OFF the button!
CRASH

MARRIAGE

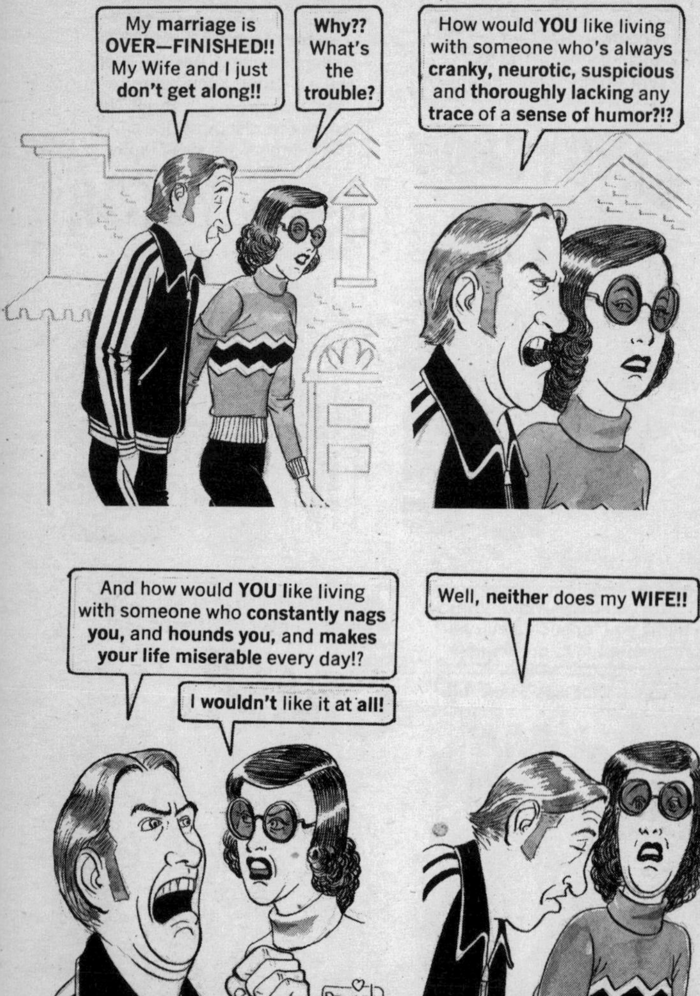

My marriage is OVER—FINISHED!! My Wife and I just don't get along!!
Why?? What's the trouble?
How would YOU like living with someone who's always cranky, neurotic, suspicious and thoroughly lacking any trace of a sense of humor?!?
And how would YOU like living with someone who constantly nags you, and hounds you, and makes your life miserable every day!?
I wouldn't like it at all!
Well, neither does my WIFE!!
David Berg

THE CAR

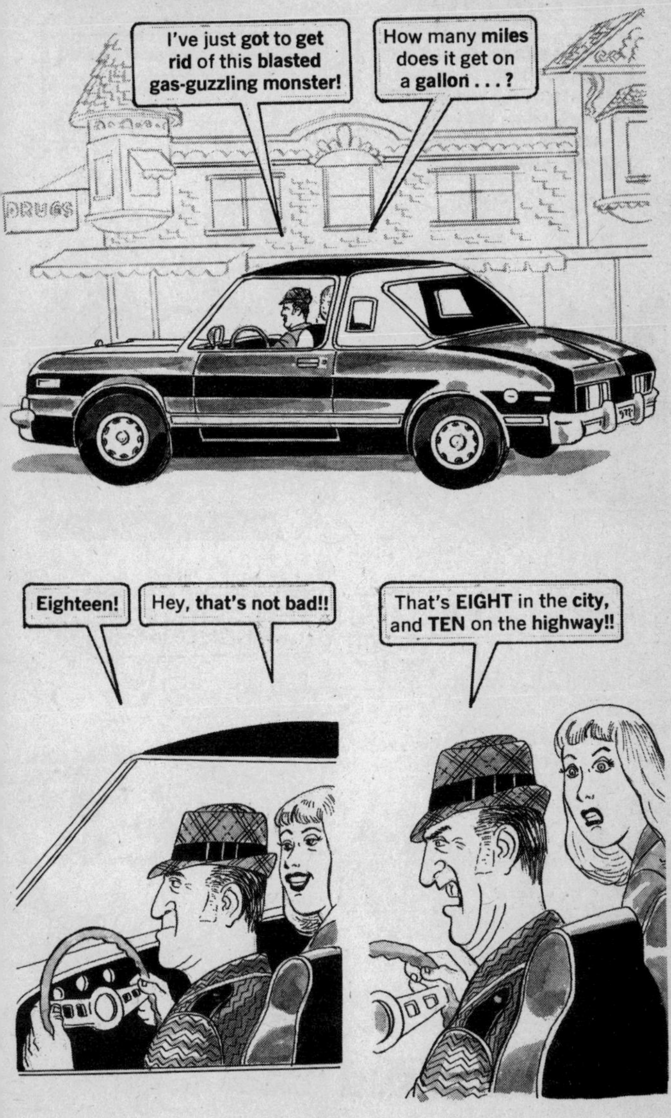

I've just got to get rid of this blasted gas-guzzling monster!
How many miles does it get on a gallon . . . ?
DRUGS
Eighteen!
Hey, that's not bad!!
That's EIGHT in the city, and TEN on the highway!!

INFLATION

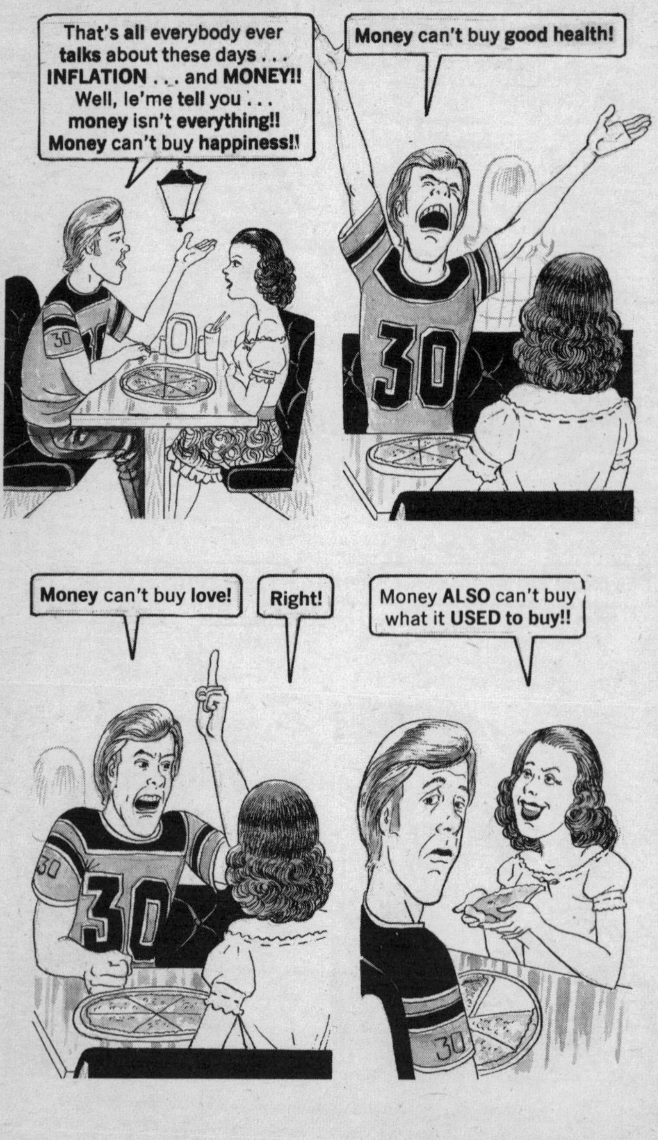
That's all everybody ever talks about these days . . . INFLATION . . . and MONEY!! Well, le'me tell you . . . money isn't everything!! Money can't buy happiness!!
Money can't buy good health!
Money can't buy love!
Right!
Money ALSO can't buy what it USED to buy!!

STYLES

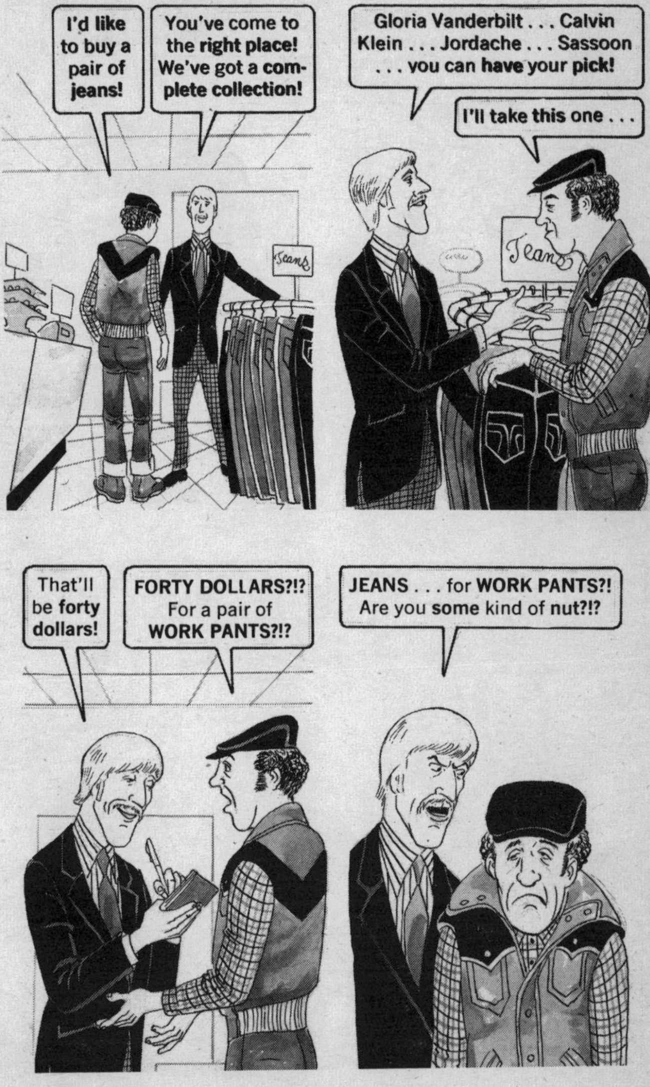
I'd like to buy a pair of jeans!
You've come to the right place! We've got a complete collection!
Gloria Vanderbilt . . . Calvin Klein . . . Jordache . . . Sassoon . . . you can have your pick!
I'll take this one . . .
Jeans
Jeans
That'll be forty dollars!
FORTY DOLLARS?!? For a pair of WORK PANTS?!?
JEANS . . . for WORK PANTS?! Are you some kind of nut?!?

EATING

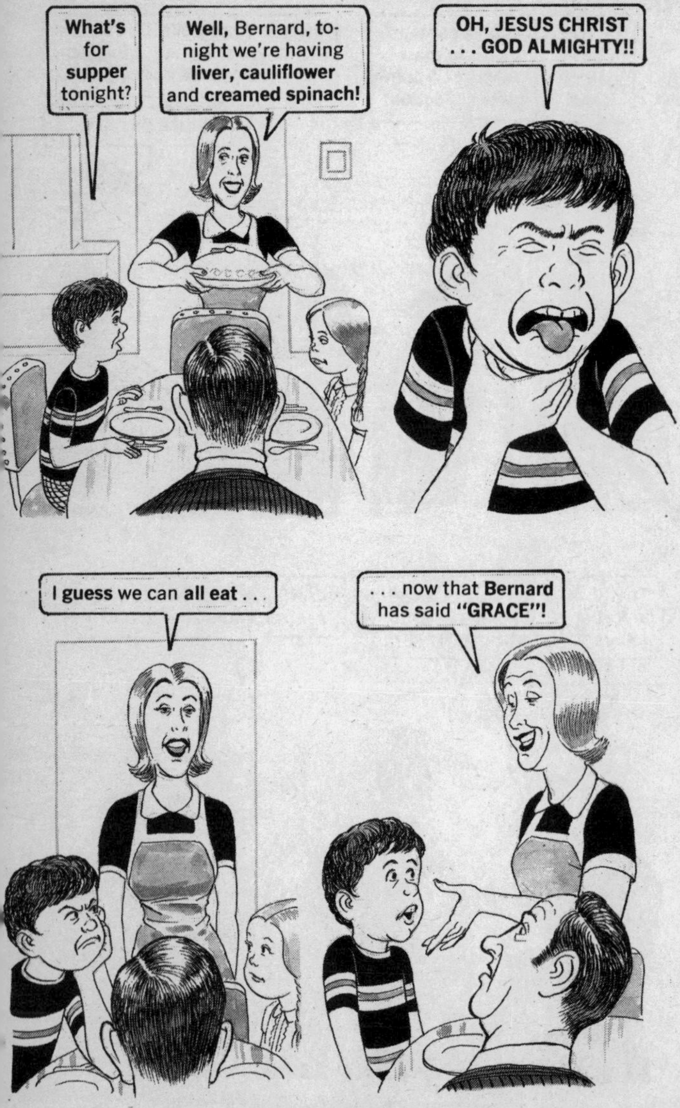
What's for supper tonight?
Well, Bernard, to-night we're having liver, cauliflower and creamed spinach!
OH, JESUS CHRIST . . . GOD ALMIGHTY!!
I guess we can all eat . . .
. . . now that Bernard has said "GRACE"!

DRESSING UP

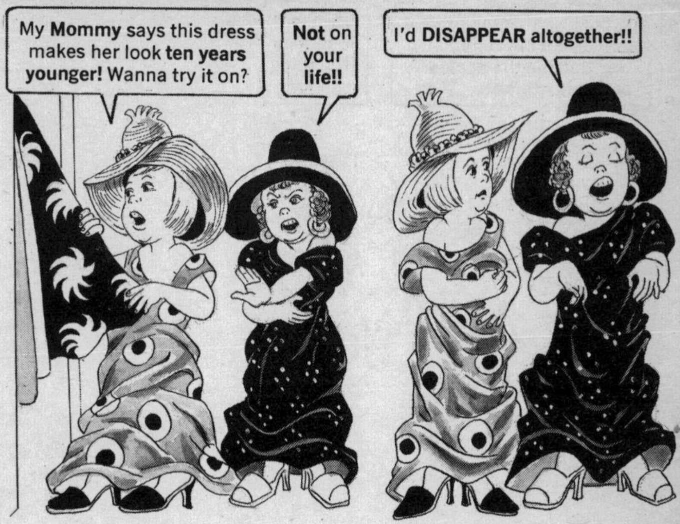
My **Mommy** says this dress makes her look **ten years younger!** Wanna try it on?
Not on your **life!!**
I'd **DISAPPEAR altogether!!**

ON THE JOB

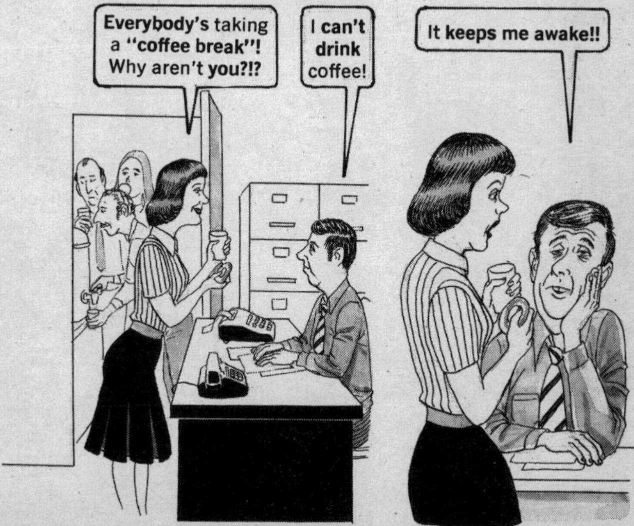
Everybody's taking a "**coffee break**"! Why aren't **you?!?**
I can't drink coffee!
It keeps me awake!!

ACTIVISTS

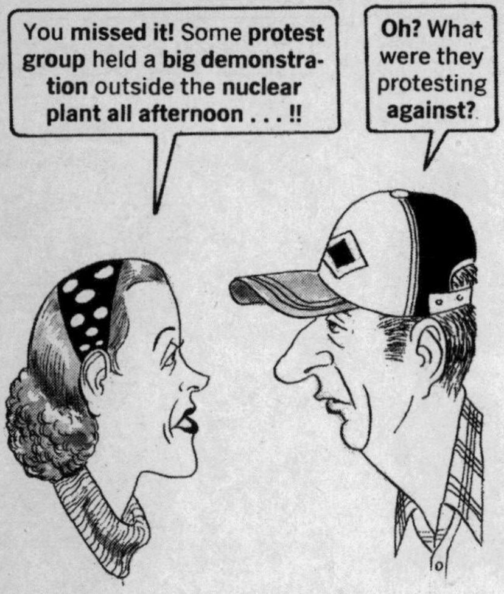

You missed it! Some protest group held a big demonstration outside the nuclear plant all afternoon . . . !!
Oh? What were they protesting against?

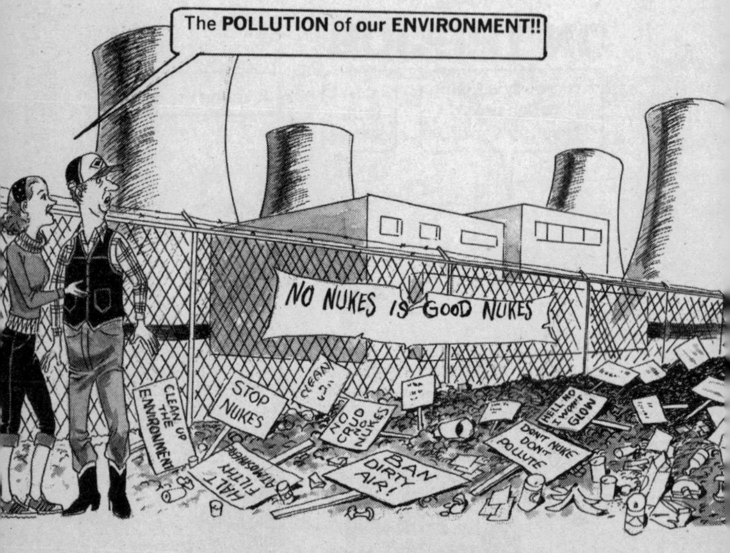

The POLLUTION of our ENVIRONMENT!!
NO NUKES IS GOOD NUKES
CLEAN UP THE ENVIRONMENT
STOP NUKES
NO CRUD NO NUKES
HELL NO I WON'T GLOW
DON'T NUKE DON'T POLLUTE
HALT FILTHY ATMOSPHERE
BAN DIRTY AIR!

JOKE AND DAGGER DEPT.

SPY vs SPY

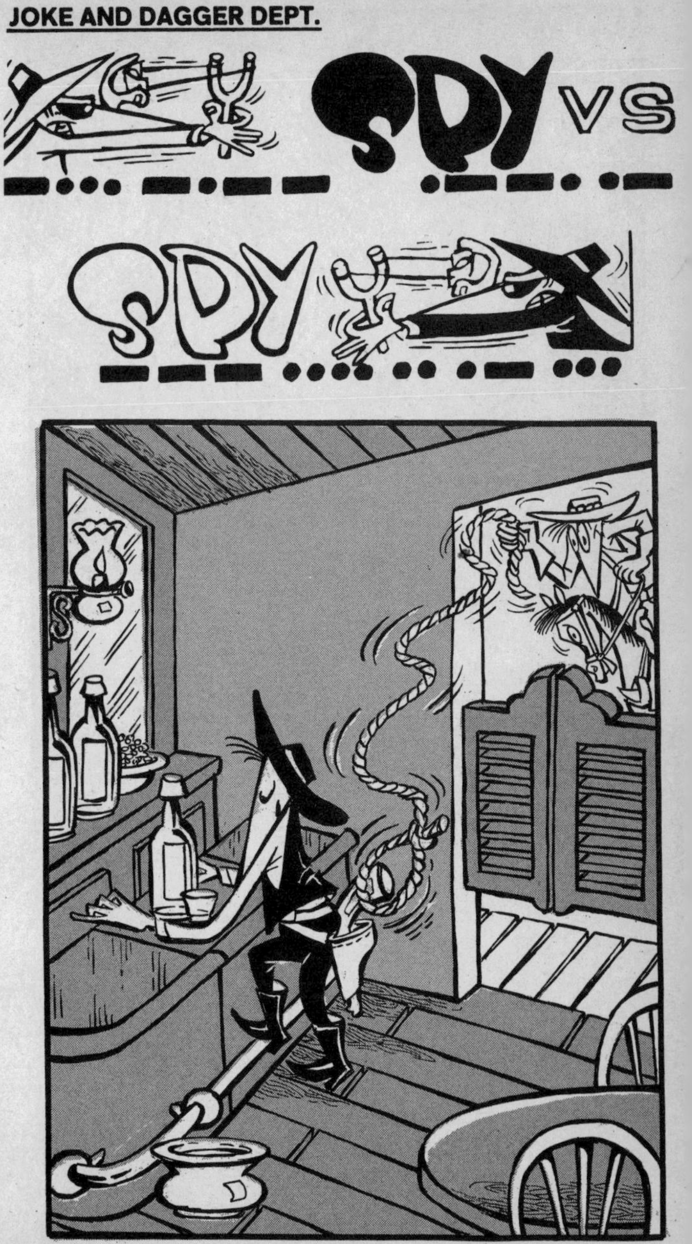

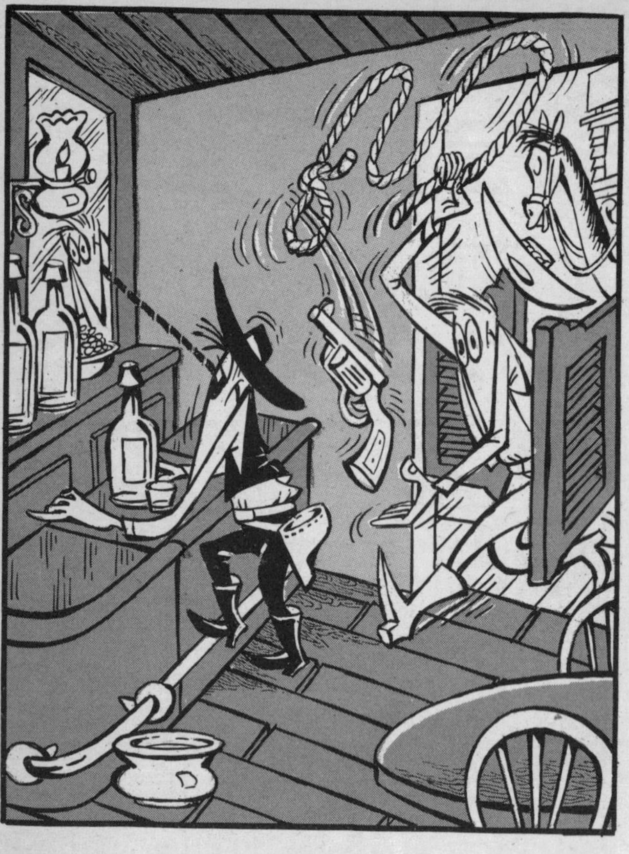

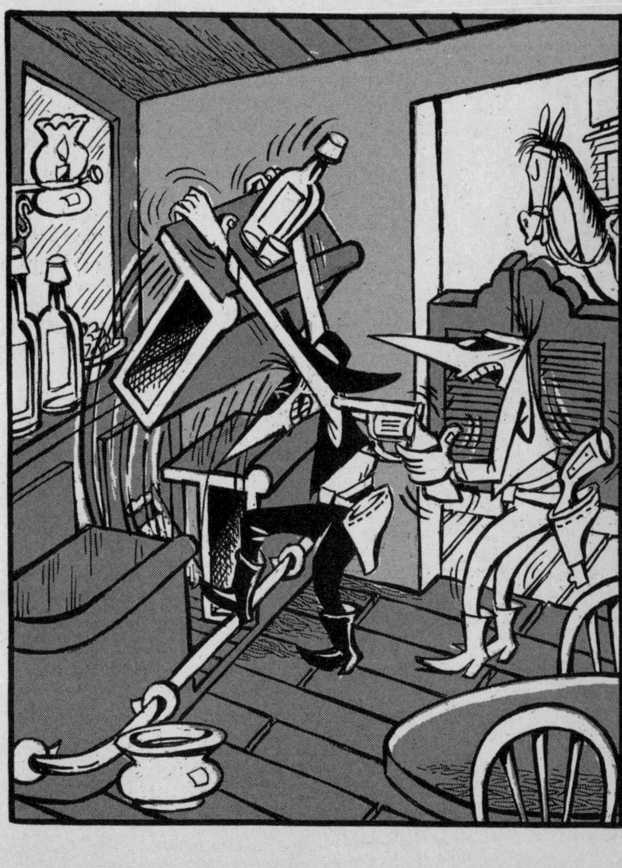

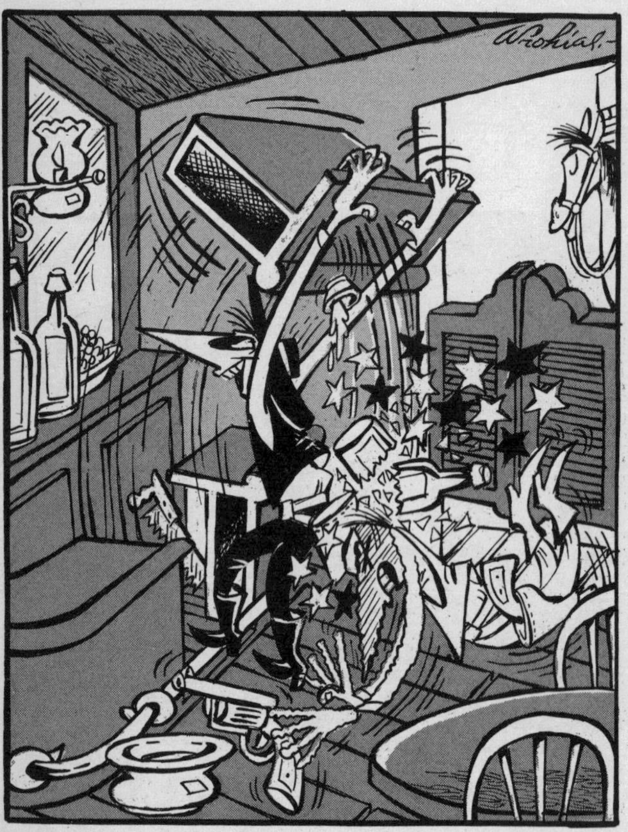

IF THEY CAN PUT A MAN ON THE MOON, THEN WHY CAN'T THEY...

ARTIST: JACK DAVIS   WRITER: JOHN FICARRA

. . . invent a parking meter that can make change of a dollar bill!?

. . . market a roll of Scotch tape that's easy to start every time!?

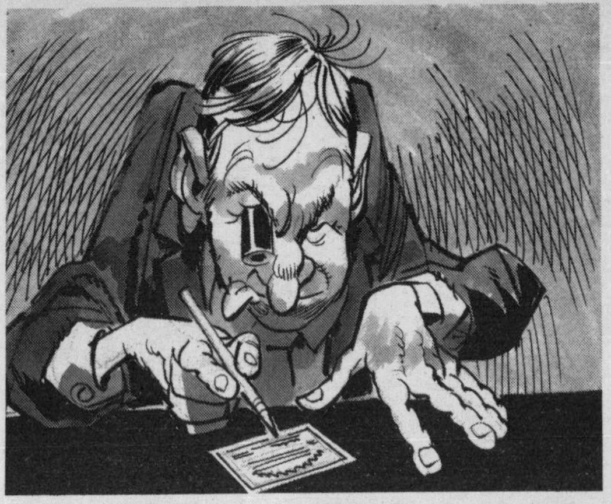

. . . design a raffle ticket that has enough space for you to write your name, address and telephone number!?

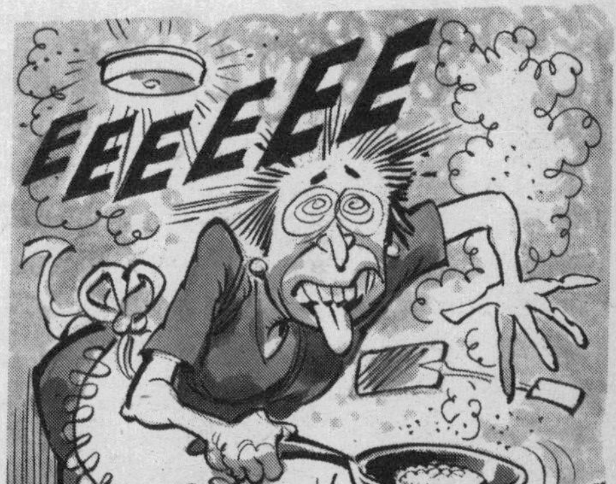
EEEEEEE

. . . invent a "Smoke Detector" that knows the difference between a real fire and a hamburger that's cooking!?

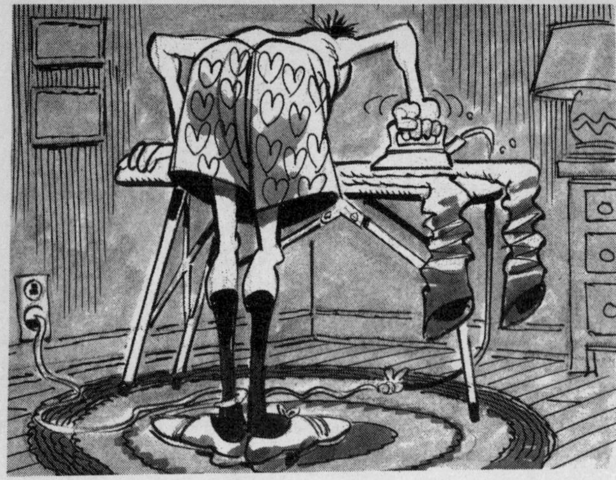

. . . make a "permanent press" garment that doesn't need touching up with a cool iron!?

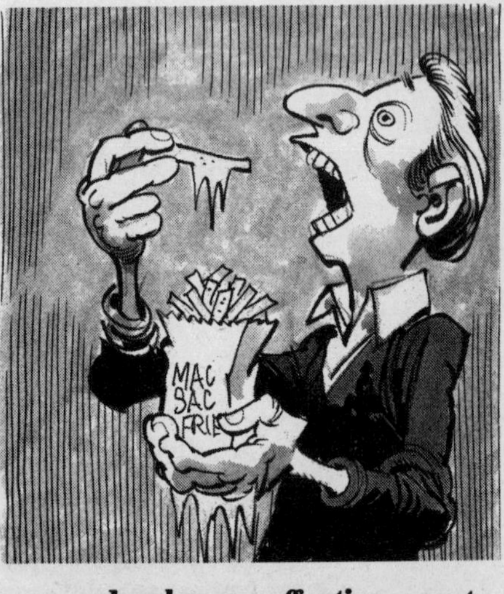
MAC
SAC
FRIE

. . . develop an effective way to keep fast-food French fries hot!?

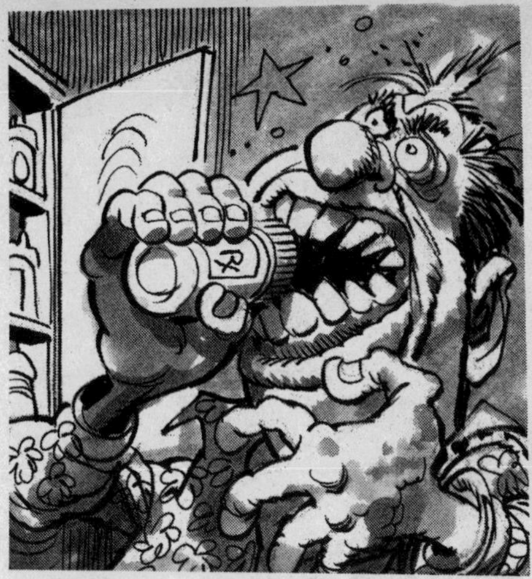
Rx

. . . devise a "child proof" medicine bottle that isn't also adult-proof!?

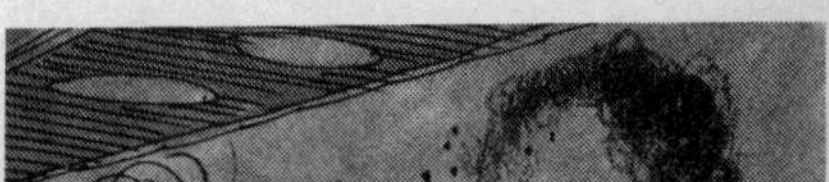
MEDIUM
LIGHT
DARK

. . . make a toaster that actually toasts the way the dial is set!?

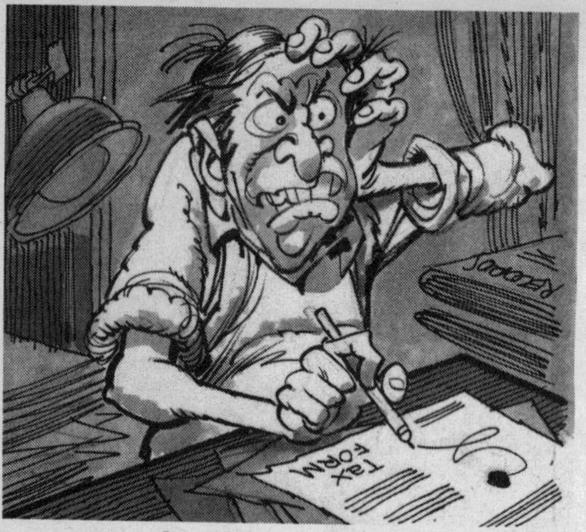
Tax FORM

. . . manufacture a ballpoint pen that doesn't leave a little blob of ink on the page whenever you start to write!?

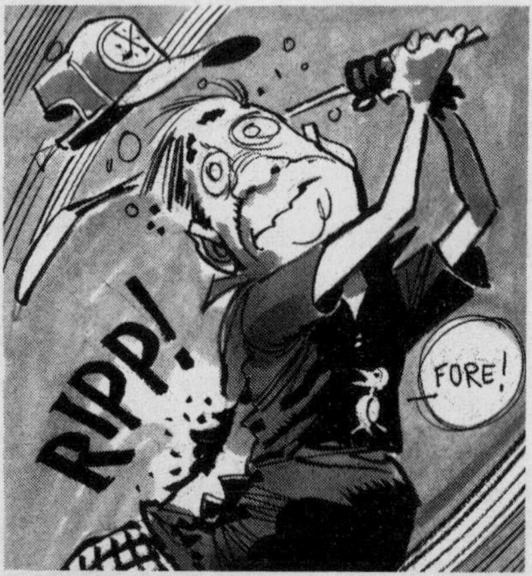
RIPP!
FORE!

. . . make a better-grade golf shirt that doesn't have a tacky little animal insignia over the pocket!?

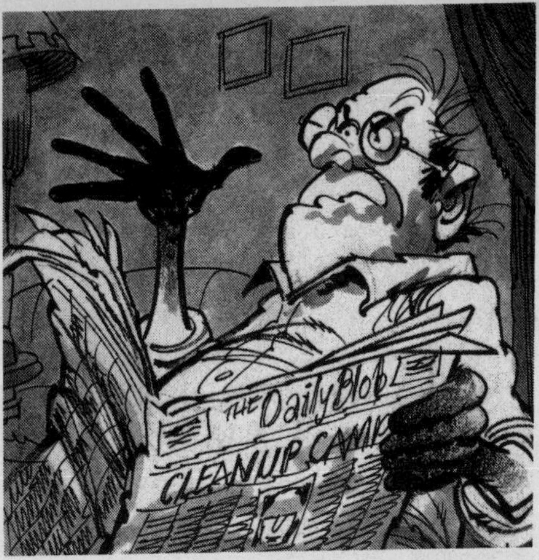
THE Daily Blob

. . . print a newspaper that doesn't make your hands black as you read!?

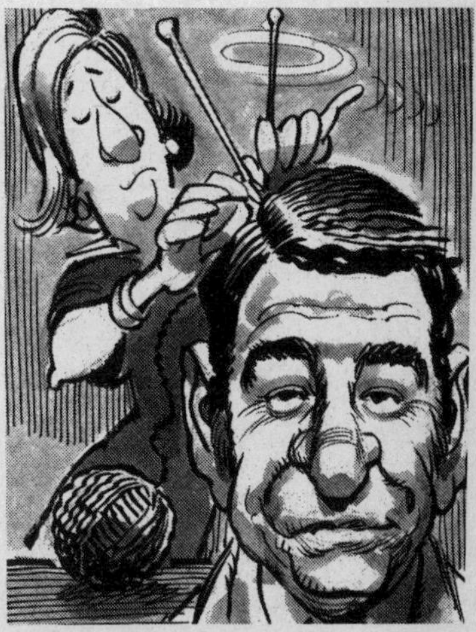

. . . knit a better-looking toupee for Howard Cosell!?

... invent an electric can opener
whose blade is easy to keep clean!?

... manufacture ice cube trays that
allow for easy removal of the cubes!?

... develop a clear plastic wrap that doesn't bunch up and cling together the second you pull it off the roll!?

... construct a picture frame that doesn't slide crooked every time someone walks by it!?

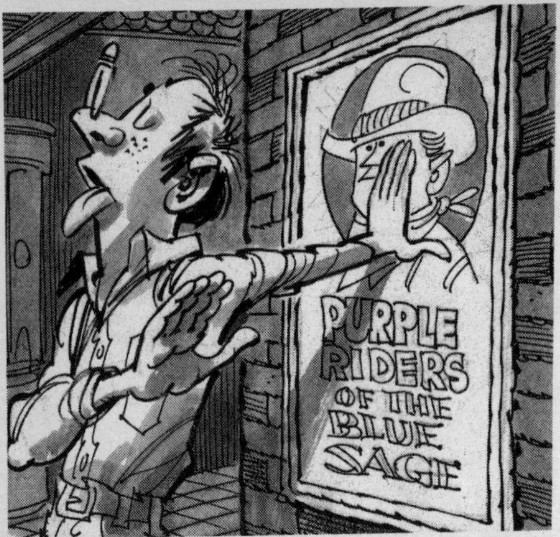
PURPLE
RIDERS
OF THE
BLUE
SAGE
. . . judge ahead of time that a motion picture or a Broadway play is a bomb!?

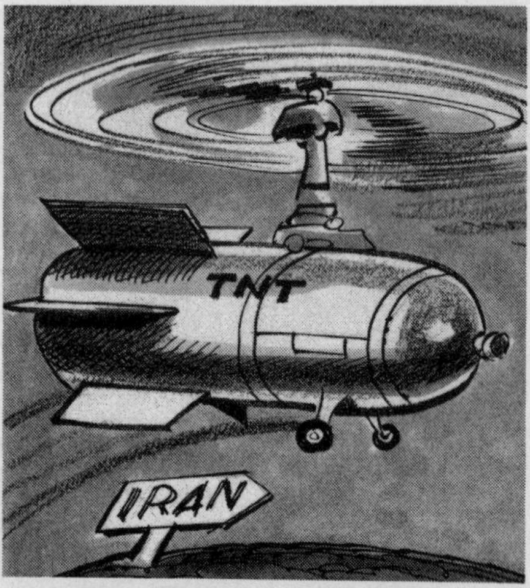
TNT
IRAN
. . . manufacture a helicopter that can actually reach Iran!?

DON MARTIN DEPT.

ONE MORNING ON A STREET CORNER

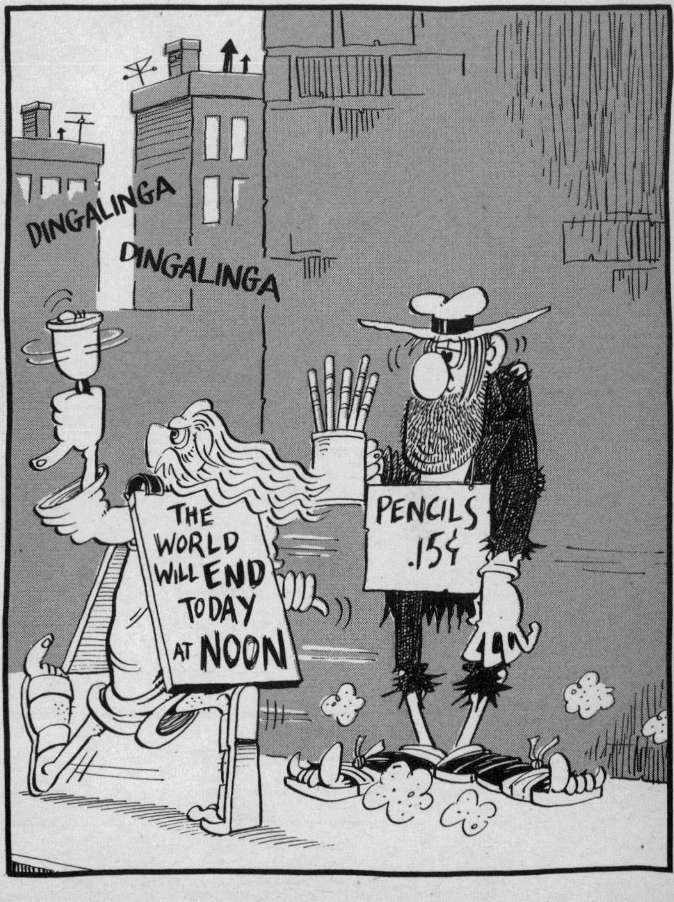
DINGALINGA
DINGALINGA
THE WORLD WILL END TODAY AT NOON
PENCILS .15¢

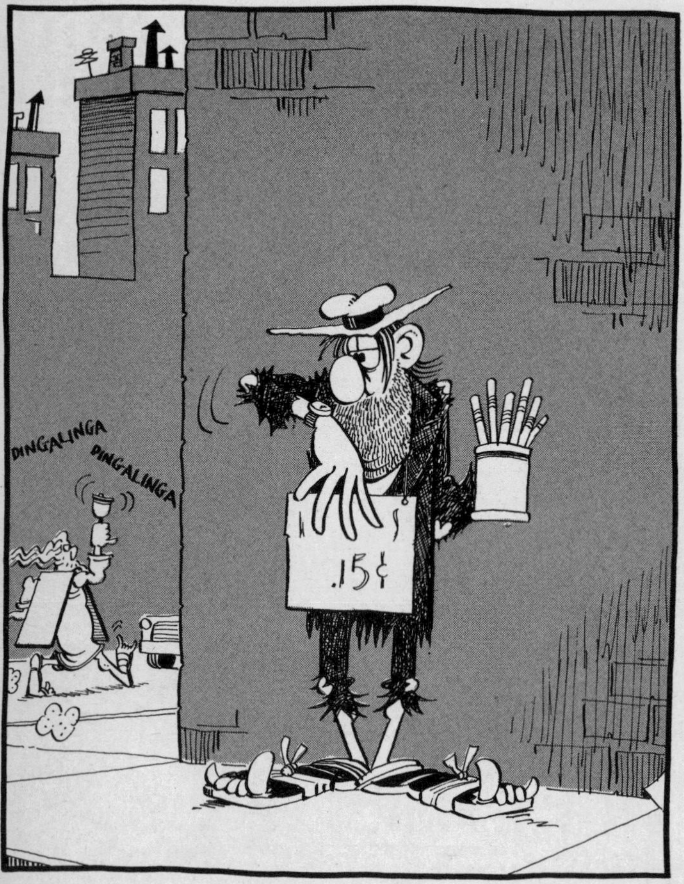
DINGALINGA
DINGALINGA
.15¢

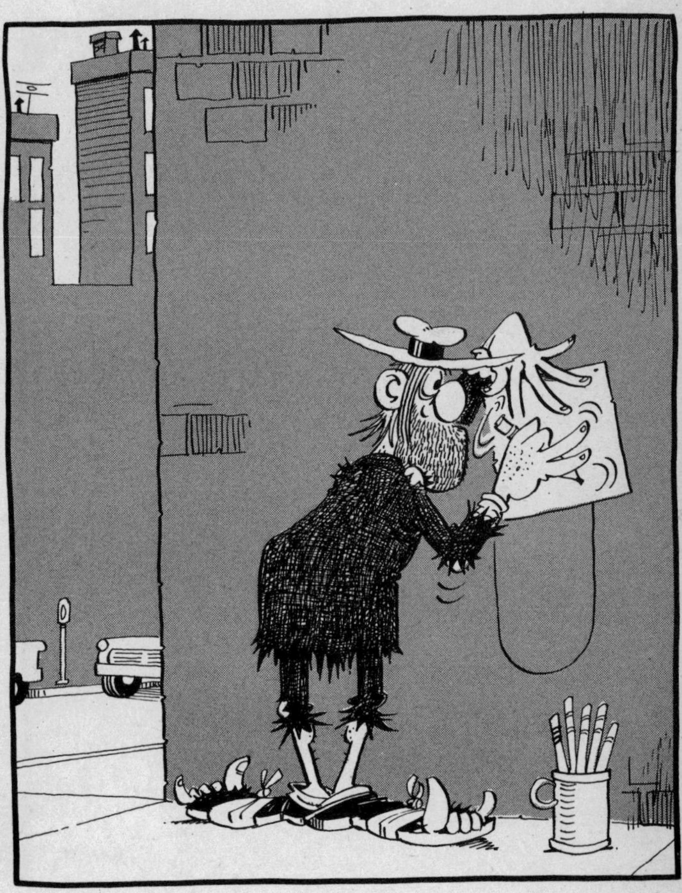

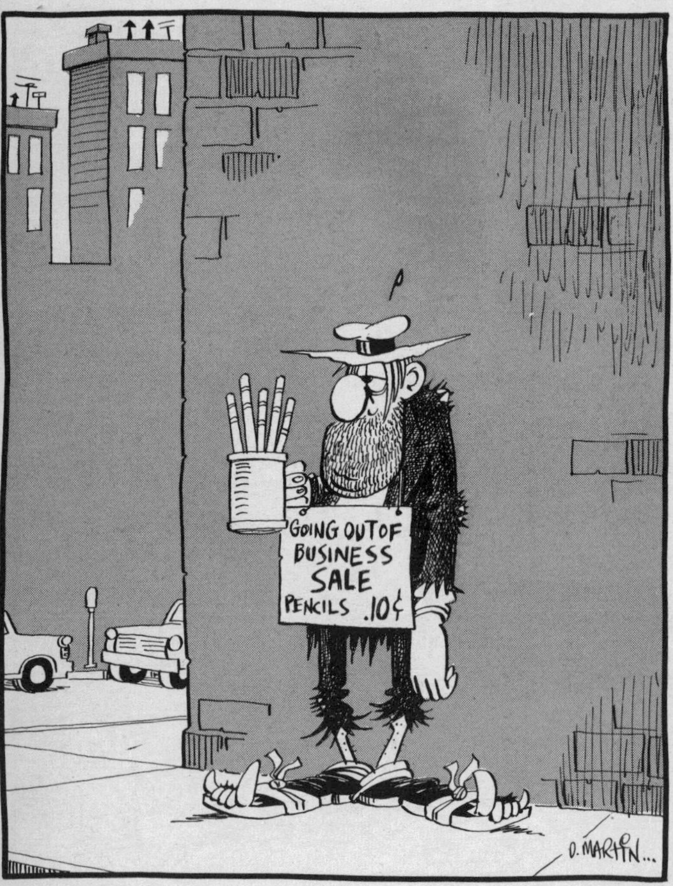
GOING OUT OF
BUSINESS
SALE
PENCILS .10¢
D. MARTIN...

GETTING IT OFF THEIR CHEST DEPT.

DID YOU REALLY THINK THE T-SHIRT CRAZE STARTED ABOUT 5 YEARS AGO? WELL, SURPRISE! IT STARTED ABOUT 5000 YEARS AGO! AND IF YOU DON'T BELIEVE US, JUST LOOK AT THESE . . .

T-SHIRTS THROUGH THE AGES

ARTIST: HARRY NORTH WRITER: DICK DE BARTOLO

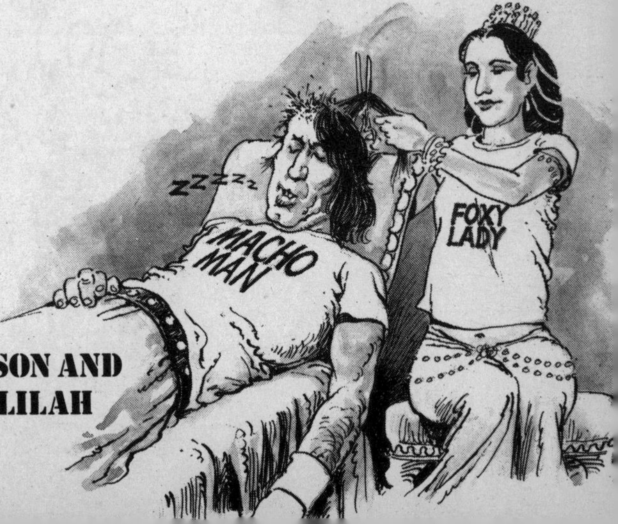
ZZZZZ
MACHO MAN
FOXY LADY

SAMSON AND DELILAH

BARON VON RICHTHOFEN

VENUS DE MILO

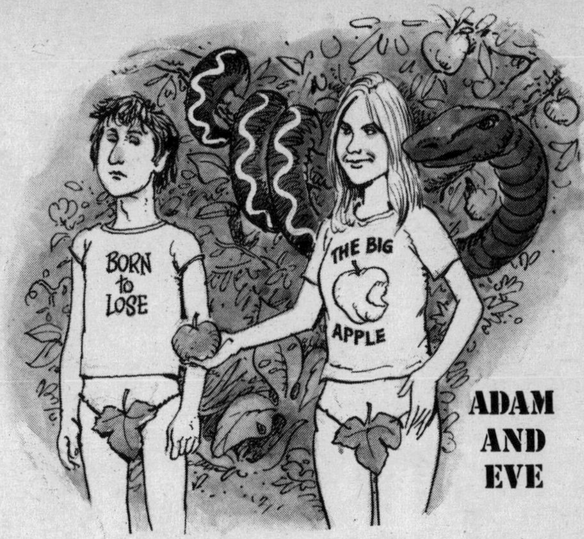
BORN to LOSE
THE BIG APPLE

ADAM AND EVE

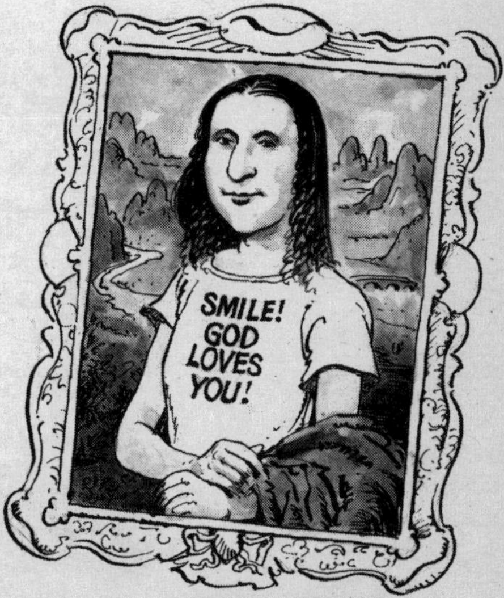
SMILE! GOD LOVES YOU!

MONA LISA

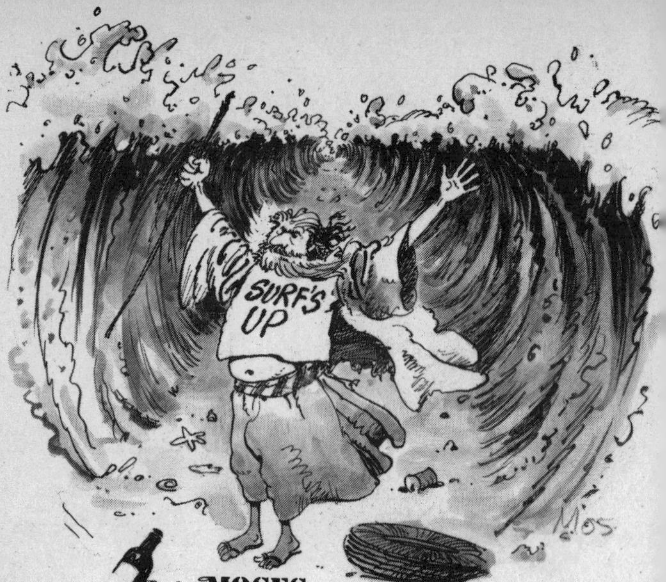
SURF'S UP
MOS

MOSES

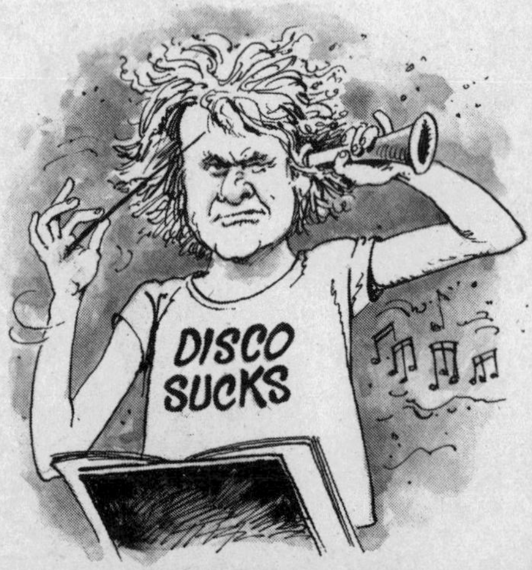
DISCO SUCKS

BEETHOVEN

KING KONG

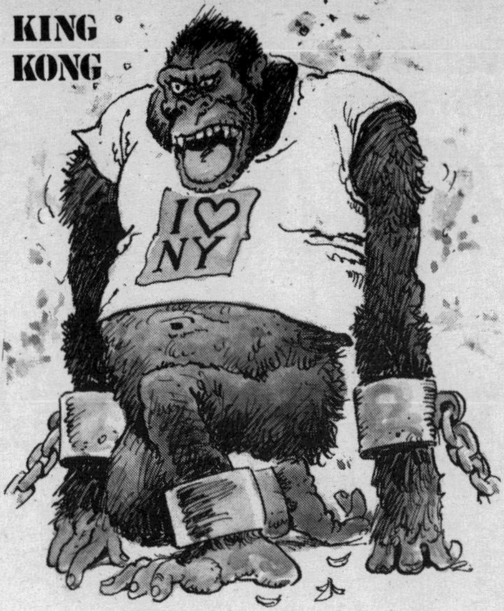
I ♥ NY

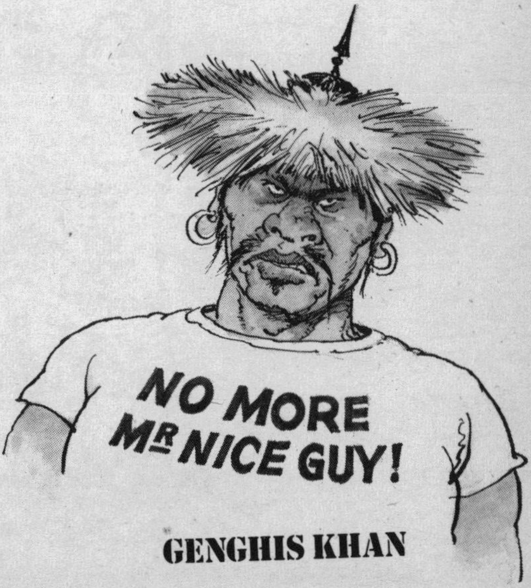
NO MORE MR NICE GUY!

GENGHIS KHAN

NAPOLEON AND JOSEPHINE

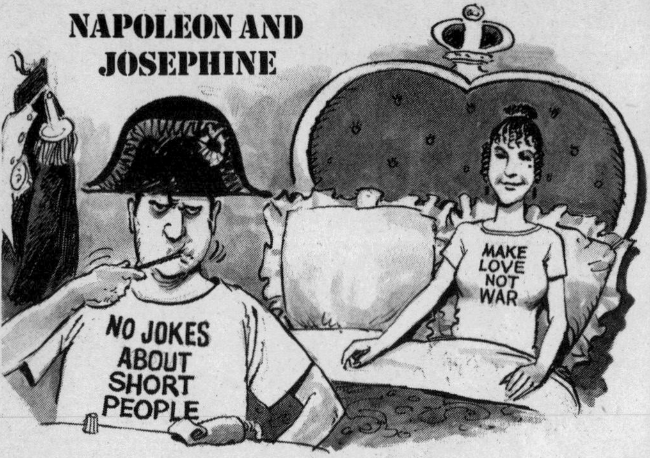
NO JOKES ABOUT SHORT PEOPLE
MAKE LOVE NOT WAR

JOAN OF ARC

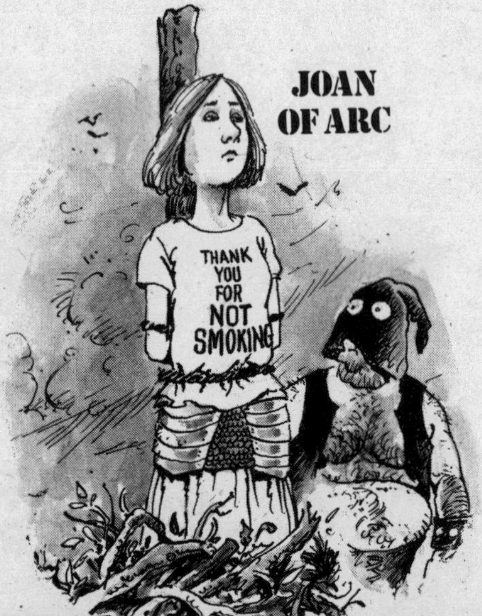
THANK YOU FOR NOT SMOKING

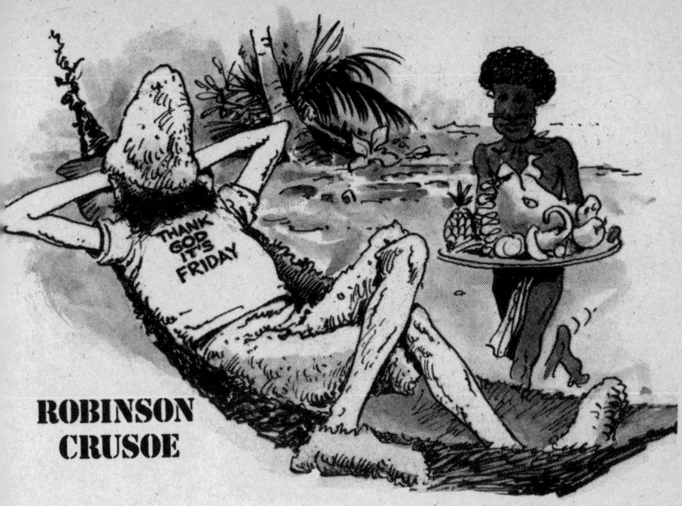
THANK GOD IT'S FRIDAY

ROBINSON CRUSOE

HENRY VIII

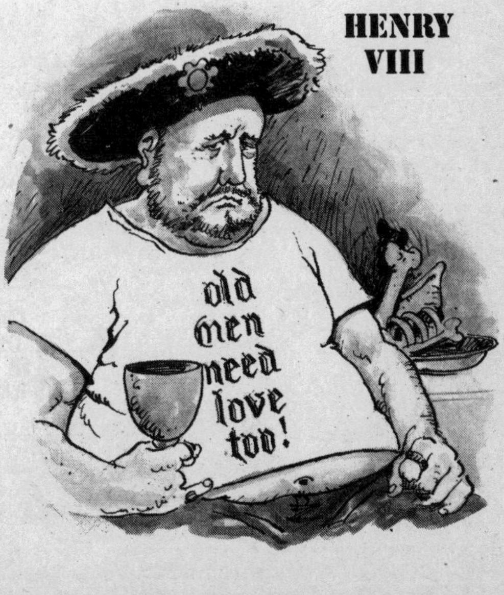
old men need love too!

TARZAN

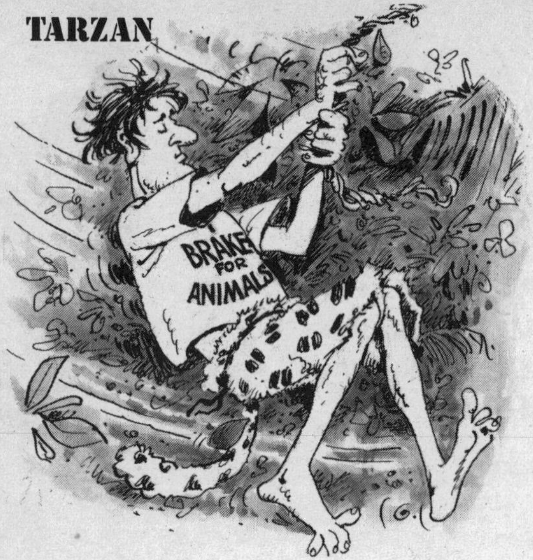
BRAKE
FOR
ANIMALS

COLUMBUS

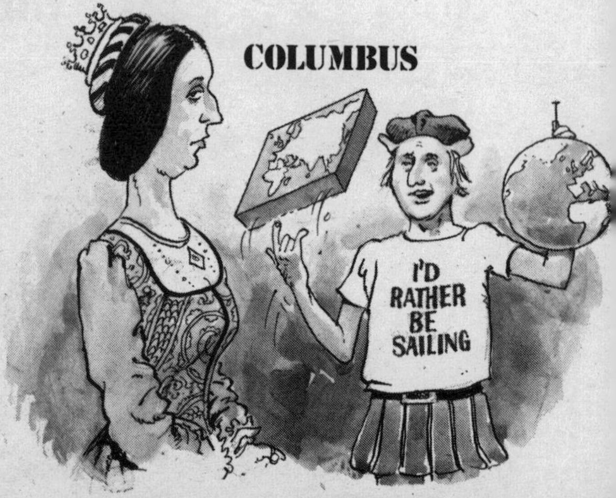
I'D
RATHER
BE
SAILING

DON MARTIN DEPT.

ONE BLAZING HOT DAY ON MAIN STREET

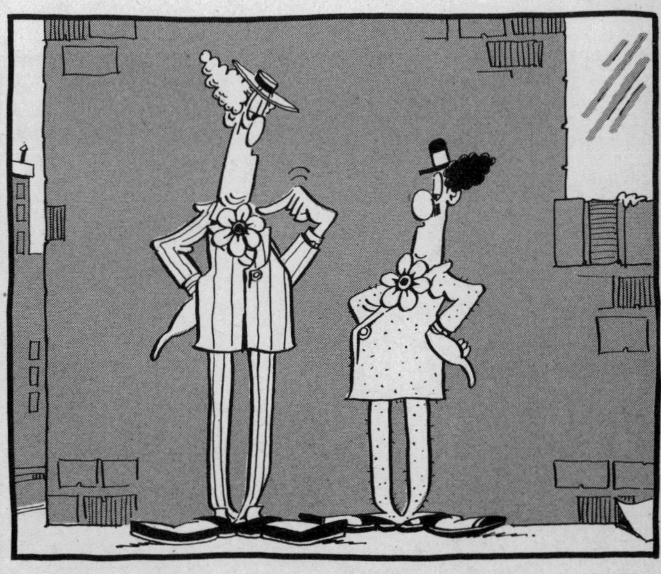

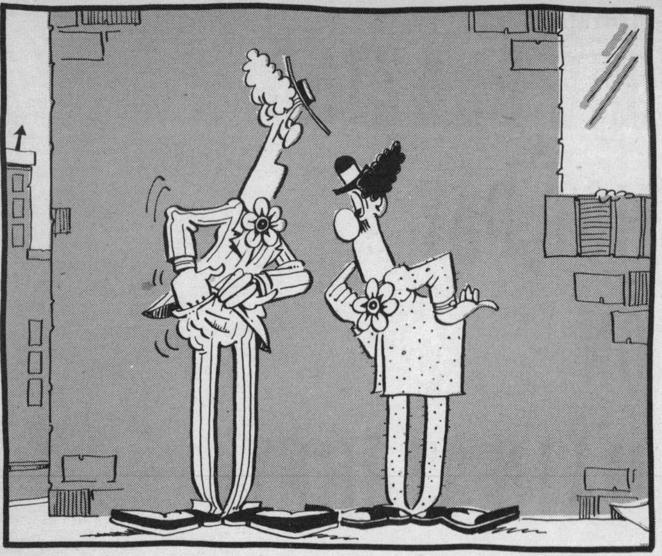

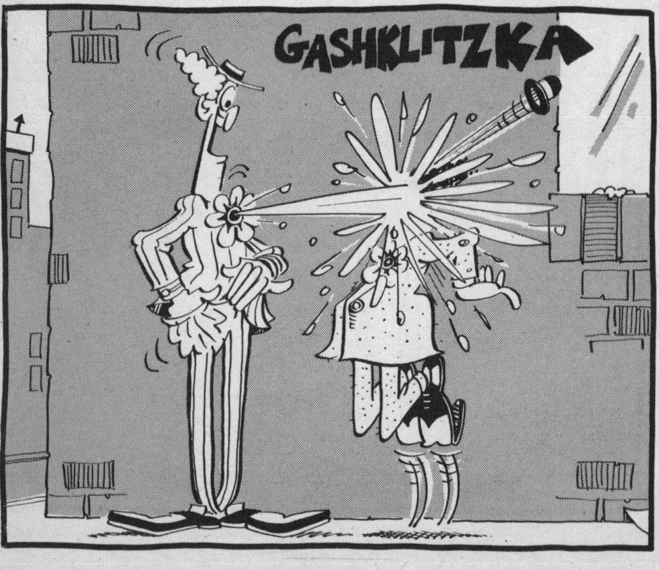
GASHKLITZKA

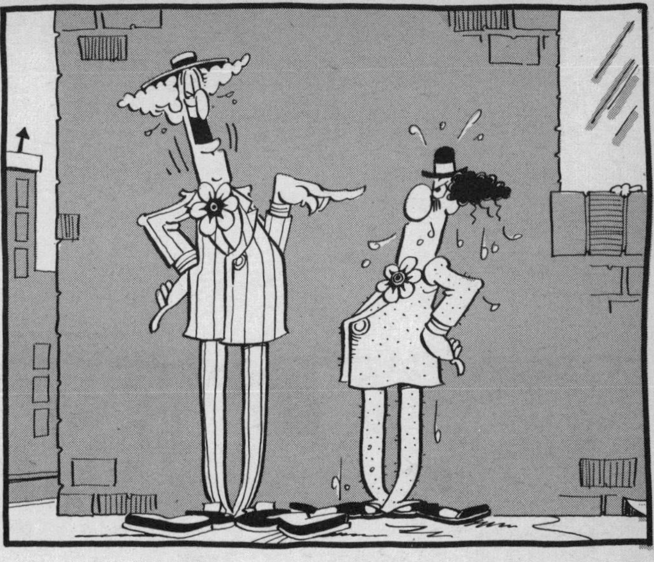

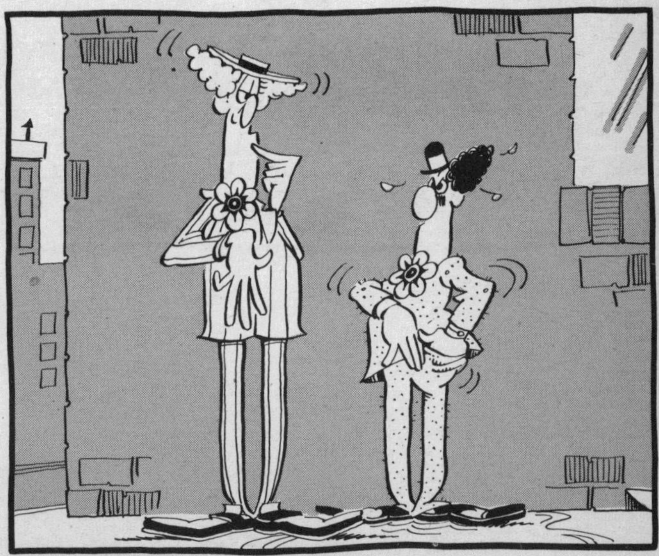

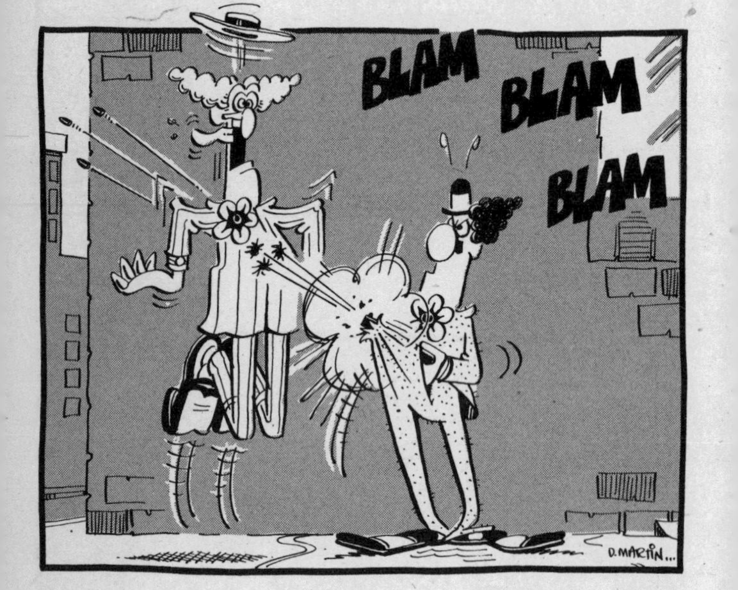
BLAM
BLAM
BLAM
D. MARTIN...

NO CONFIDENCE GAME DEPT.

HOW CAN YOU POSSIBLY BELIEVE...

ARTIST: PAUL COKER WRITER: GEORGE HART

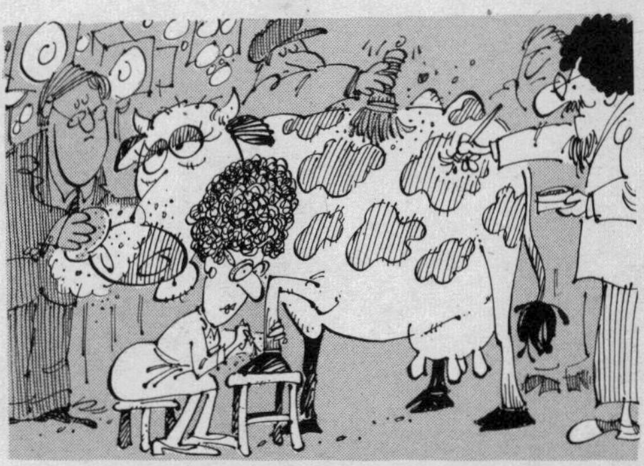

. . . TV ads that tell you how wonderful milk is . . when they're paid for by the American Dairy Council!

... a Doctor who advises you to stop smoking ... with a full ash tray on his desk!

... a Health Food Store clerk ...
who looks like death warmed over!

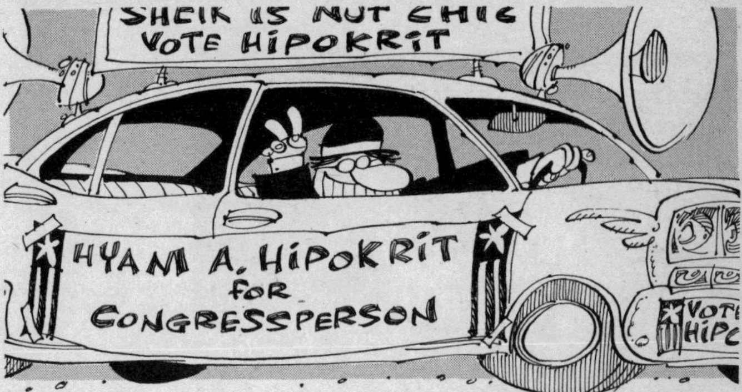
SHEIK IS NOT CHIC
VOTE HIPOKRIT
HYAM A. HIPOKRIT
FOR
CONGRESSPERSON

. . . a Politician who preaches energy conservation . . . and drives a big gas guzzler!

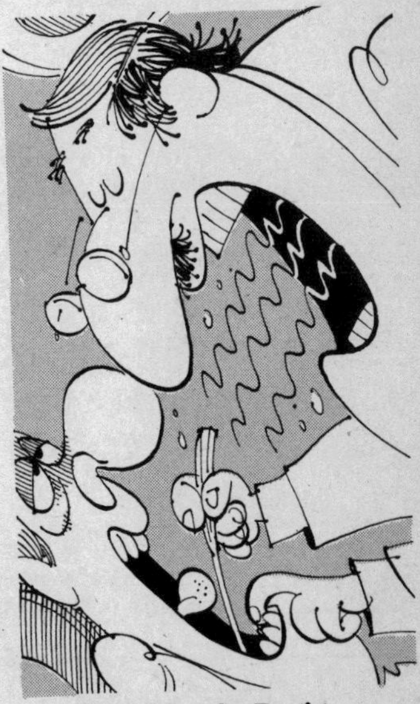

**. . . the advice of a Dentist . . .
who has (yecch) Denture Breath!**

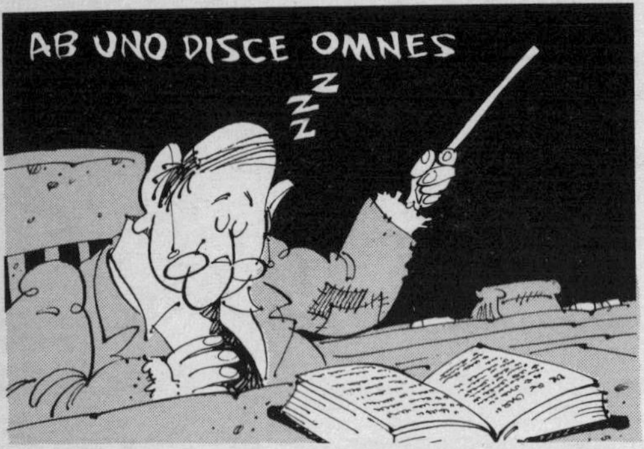
AB UNO DISCE OMNES
ZZZ

. . . that mastery of a school subject will help you to rise to the top of your chosen field . . . when it's told to you by a teacher who's been in the same dead-end job for 30 years!

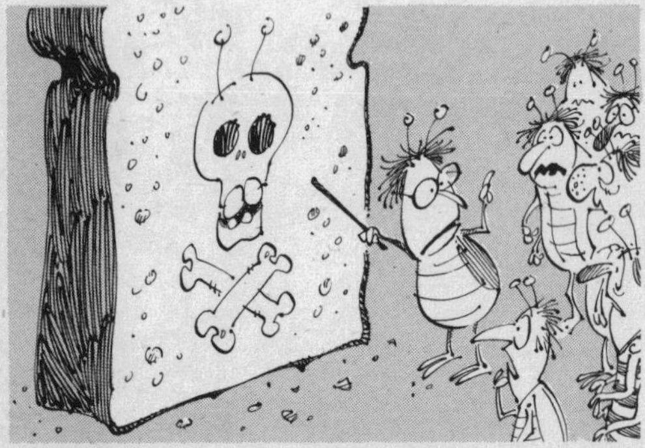

. . . that white bread can "build strong bodies ten ways". . . when it's so filled with chemicals, even bugs won't eat it!

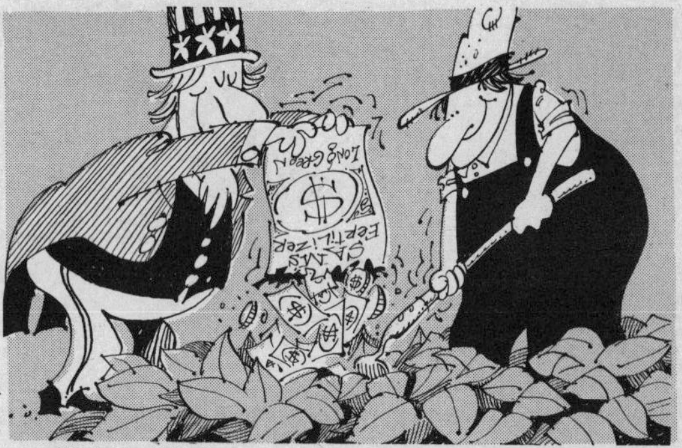
LONG GREEN
SAM'S
FERTILIZER

. . . the United States Government, when it tells you smoking cigarettes is deadly . . . and then subsidizes tobacco growers!

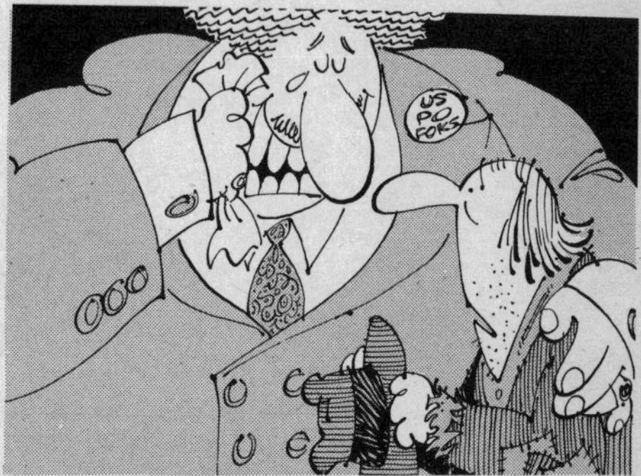
US
PO
FOKS

. . . a Senator who's been wealthy all his life . . . and claims that he understands the problems of the poor!

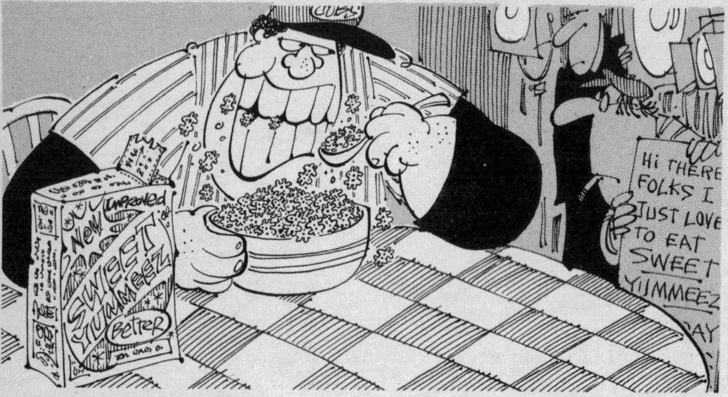
New Improved
SWEET YUMMEEZ
Better
HI THERE FOLKS I JUST LOVE TO EAT SWEET YUMMEEZ

. . . a commercial by a top star . . . when you read he got paid $150,000 to make it!

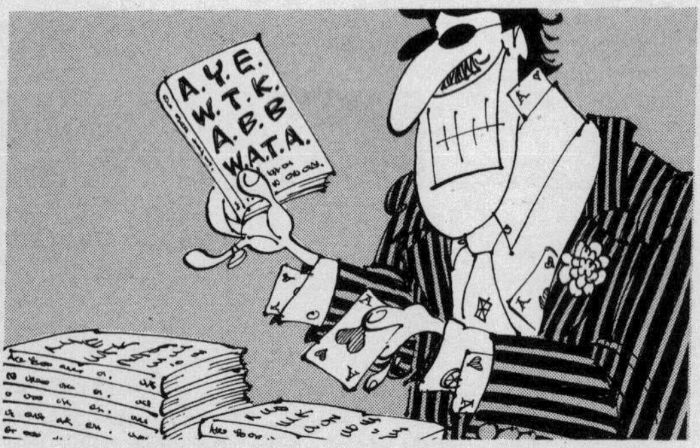
A.Y.E.
W.T.K.
A.B.B.
W.A.T.A.

. . . a guy who spends all his time selling a $10 course on "How To Get Rich Playing Blackjack". . . instead of going to Las Vegas and getting rich that way himself!

DON MARTIN DEPT.

LATE ONE EVENING ON DEATH ROW

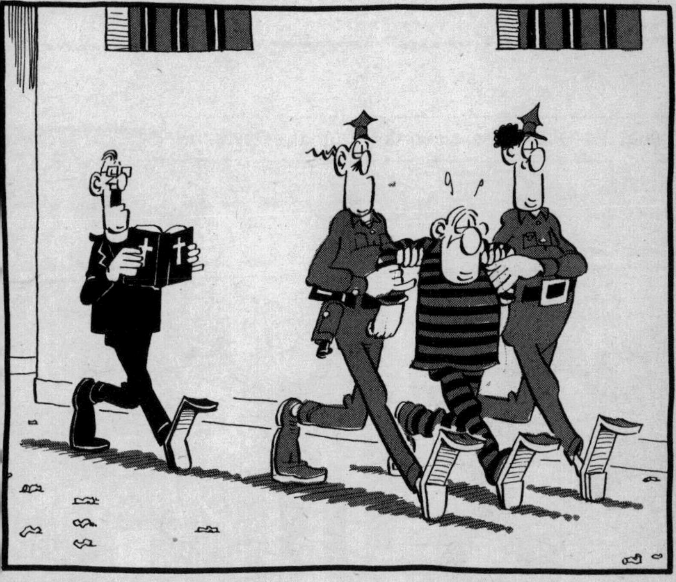

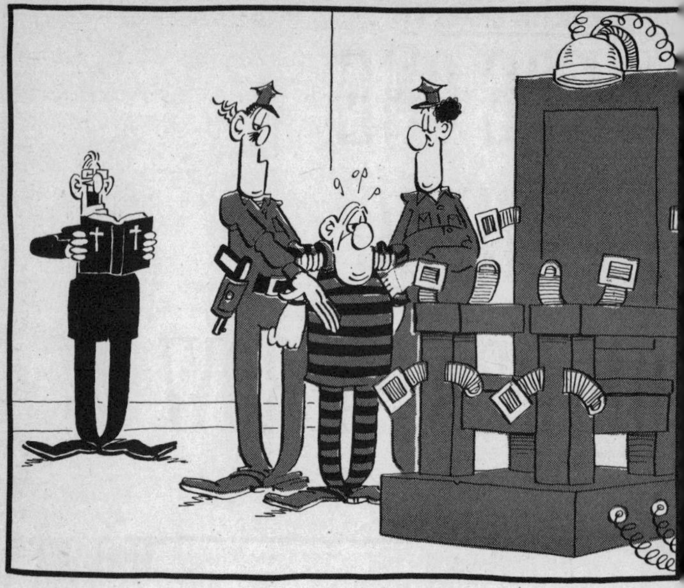

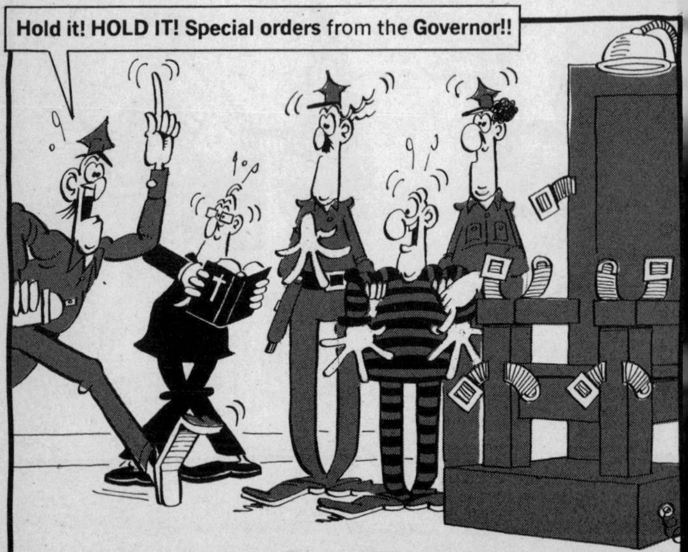
Hold it! HOLD IT! Special orders from the Governor!!

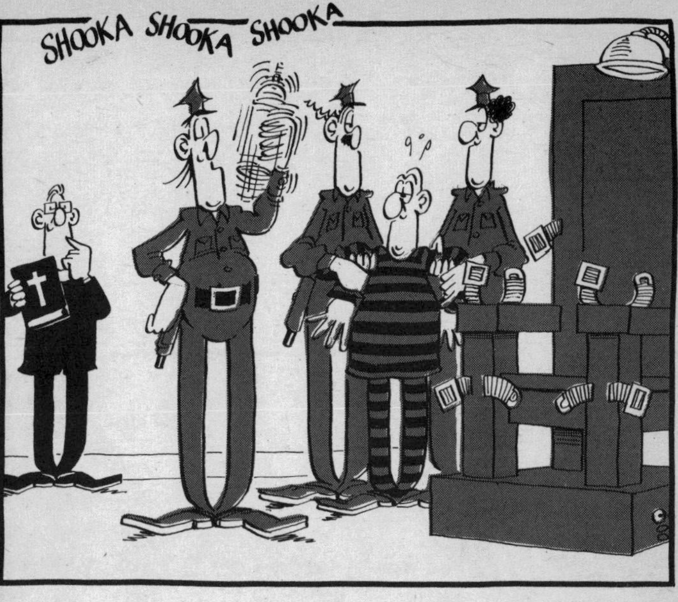
SHOOKA SHOOKA SHOOKA

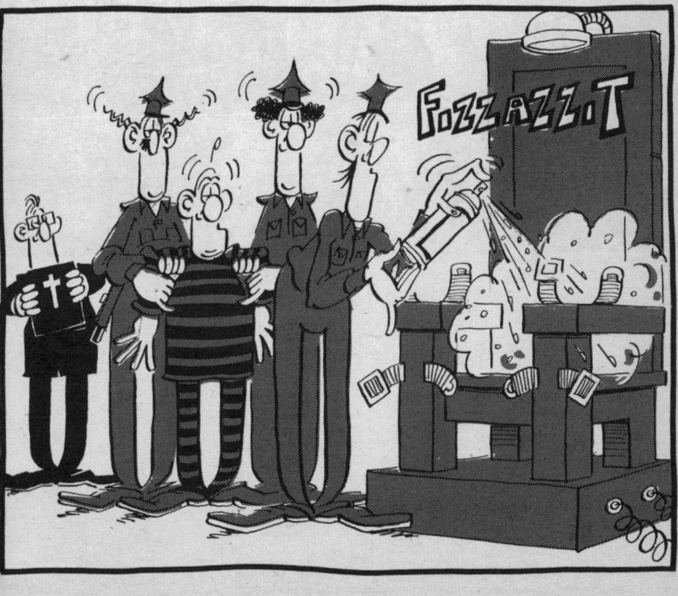
FOZZAZZ.T

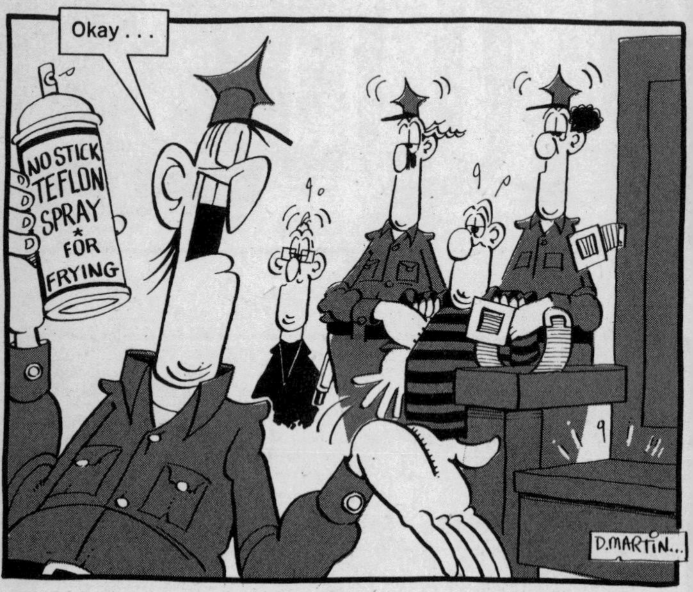
Okay . . .
NO STICK TEFLON SPRAY * FOR FRYING
D.MARTIN...

No matter how many new laws the Government passes, and no matter how many new Agencies they set up to protect us gullible consumers from Madison Avenue...

WE'LL ALWAYS BE SUCKERS FOR CLEVER ADVERTISING...

ARTIST: JACK RICKARD   WRITER: TOM KOCH

WE'LL ALWAYS BE SUCKERS FOR CLEVER ADVERTISING

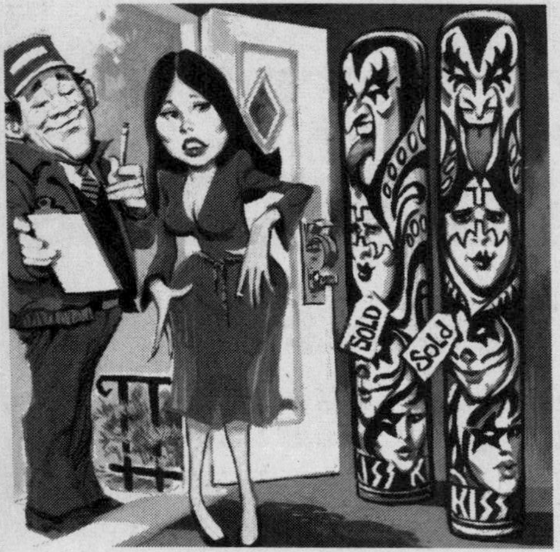
SOLD
Sold
KISS
KISS

. . . because invitations to "buy one, get the second one free" sound so appealing, we quickly forget we can't even use one!

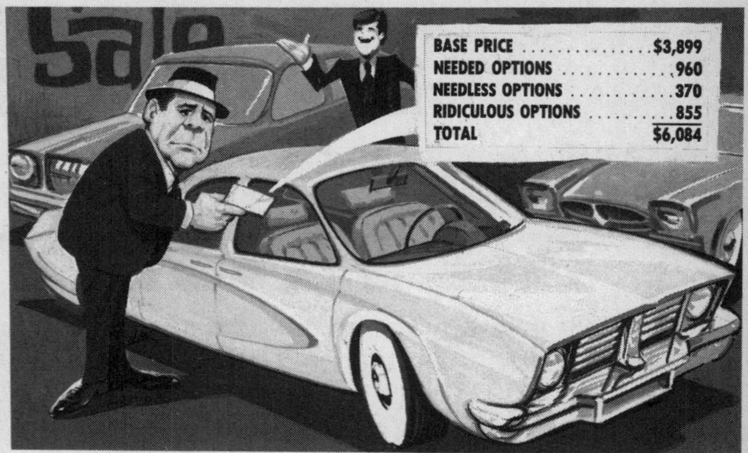
Sale
BASE PRICE $3,899
NEEDED OPTIONS 960
NEEDLESS OPTIONS 370
RIDICULOUS OPTIONS 855
TOTAL $6,084

. . . because we're already inside the dealer's showroom with our tongues hanging out before we realize that $3,899 cars really cost over $6,000 by the time wheels, windows and other "optional equipment" are added in.

WE'LL ALWAYS BE SUCKERS FOR CLEVER ADVERTISING

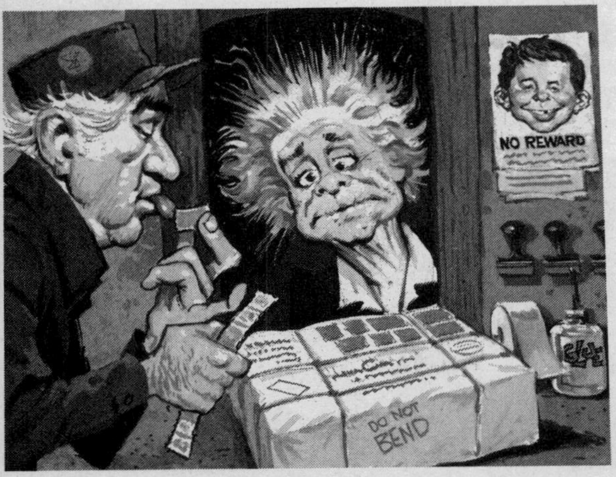
NO REWARD
DO NOT BEND

. . . because we don't find out until too late that it costs less to keep the junk we buy from mail order houses than it does to pay the postage to return it.

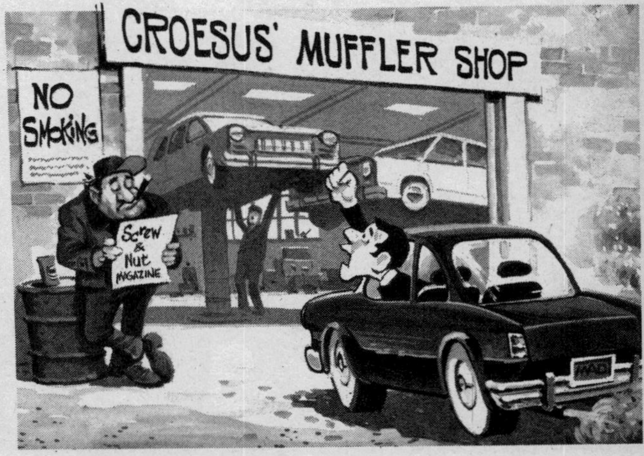
CROESUS' MUFFLER SHOP
NO SMOKING
Screw & Nut MAGAZINE
MAD

. . . because we're lured to muffler shops that offer "30-Minute Service," even though we know it takes longer than that just to get a mechanic's attention.

WE'LL ALWAYS BE SUCKERS FOR CLEVER ADVERTISING

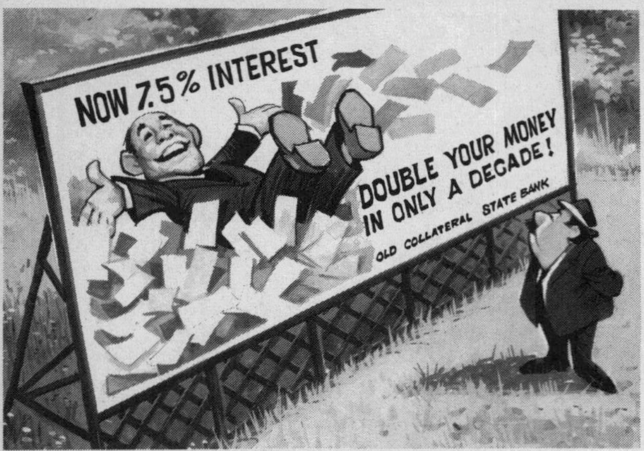
NOW 7.5% INTEREST
DOUBLE YOUR MONEY IN ONLY A DECADE!
OLD COLLATERAL STATE BANK

. . . because banks don't remind us that we could also have doubled our money in the past ten years investing in light bulbs, blue jeans, shoes or kitty litter.

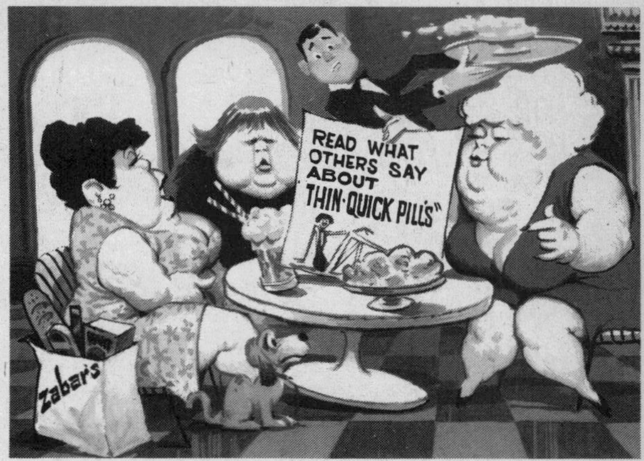
READ WHAT OTHERS SAY ABOUT THIN·QUICK PILLS"
Zabar's

. . . because it impresses us to read how "Mrs. J. M. of California" has praised a product, even though we have no idea who she is, or if she even exists.

WE'LL ALWAYS BE SUCKERS FOR CLEVER ADVERTISING

... because a TV announcer with a British accent has a way of making even worthless trash sound like high-quality merchandise.

DOMESTIC RAYON SINGLE-KNIT $125.95

FINE TIMEPIECES $21.95 (and up)

... because they deviously bunch items of different prices together, hoping we'll think the one we want is cheap.

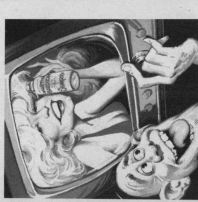

... because we stupidly assume that anything sold by Farrah Fawcett-Majors has to be great.

WE'LL ALWAYS BE SUCKERS FOR CLEVER ADVERTISING

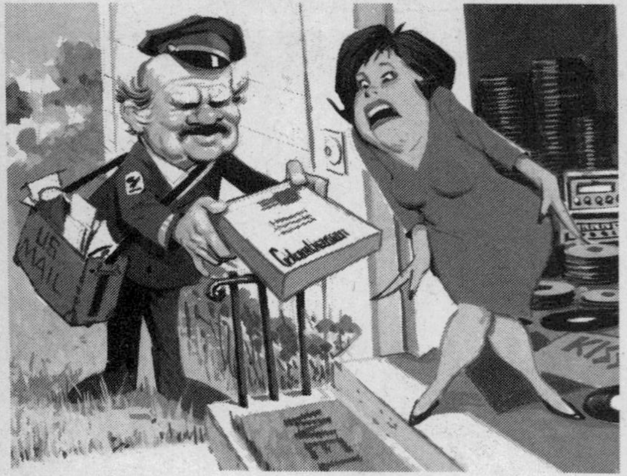
US MAIL
WEL
KISS

. . . because a chance to get ten free albums for joining a record club blinds us to the fact that there's no way we can drop out once we've joined.

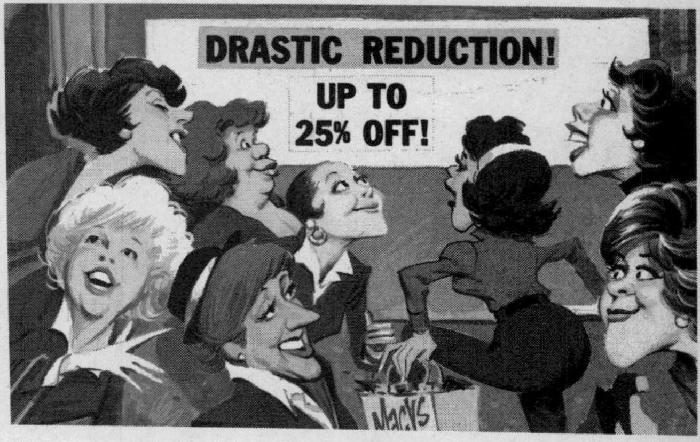
DRASTIC REDUCTION!
UP TO
25% OFF!
MACY'S

. . . because hardly anybody remembers that the sales items "drastically reduced" from $89.00 to $69.00 are the same ones that were drastically increased from $49.00 last year.

WE'LL ALWAYS BE SUCKERS FOR CLEVER ADVERTISING

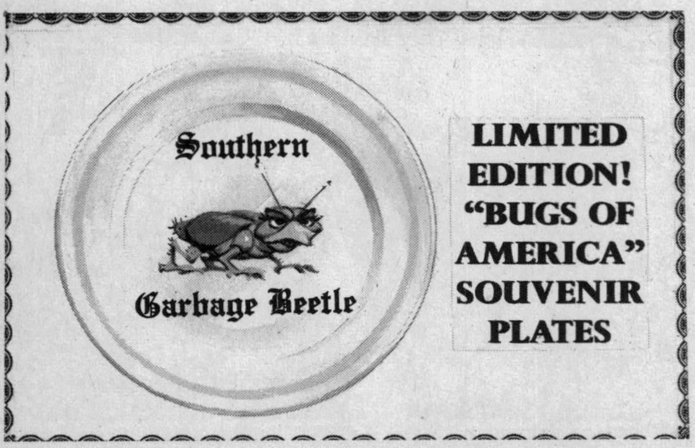
Southern
Garbage Beetle
LIMITED
EDITION!
"BUGS OF
AMERICA"
SOUVENIR
PLATES

. . . because few realize that "a collector's item much in demand" will stop being in demand as soon as every collector orders his from the same ad we're reading.

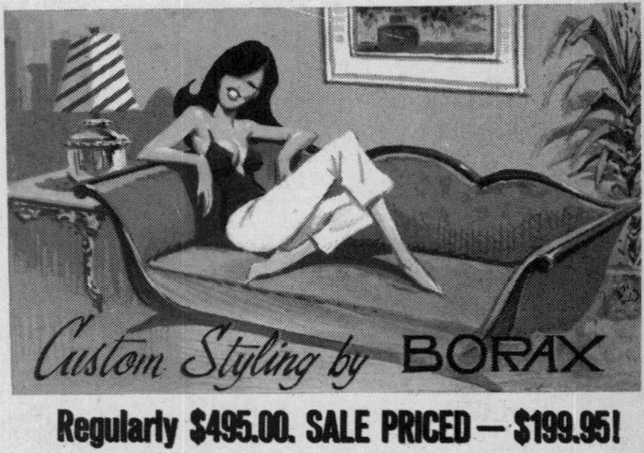
Custom Styling by BORAX
Regularly $495.00. SALE PRICED — $199.95!

. . . because draping a beautiful model across cheap furniture makes any sofa look much better in the ad than it's ever going to look in our living room.

WE'LL ALWAYS BE SUCKERS FOR CLEVER ADVERTISING

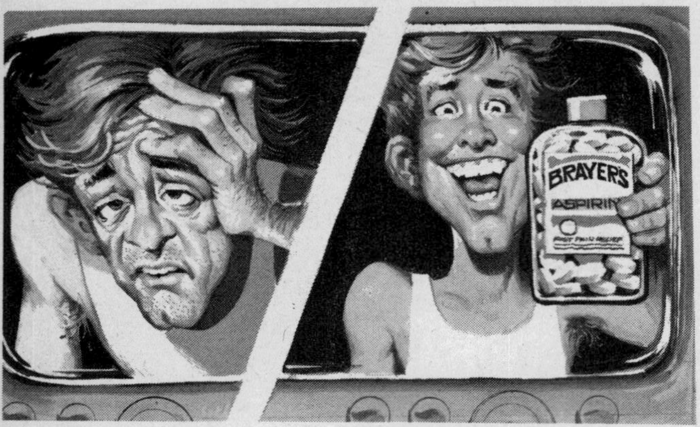
BRAYER'S
ASPIRIN

. . . because we invariably buy pills promising "temporary relief from minor pain" after we see how they provide the actor in the commercial with permanent relief from major pain.

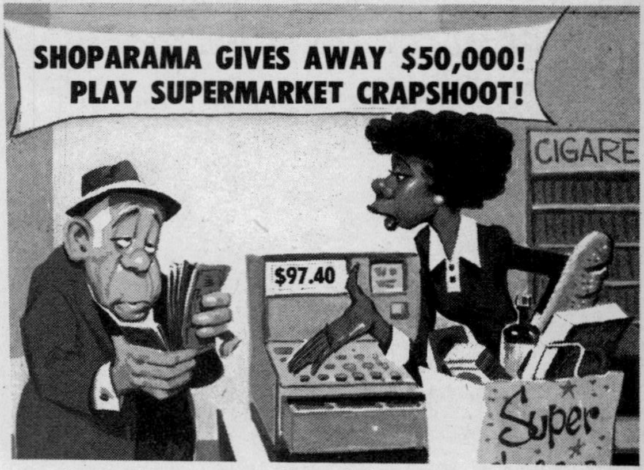
SHOPARAMA GIVES AWAY $50,000!
PLAY SUPERMARKET CRAPSHOOT!
CIGARE
$97.40
Super

. . . because supermarkets promoting those sweepstake games act as if the prize money is coming out of their profits . . . and not your pockets.

WE'LL ALWAYS BE SUCKERS FOR CLEVER ADVERTISING

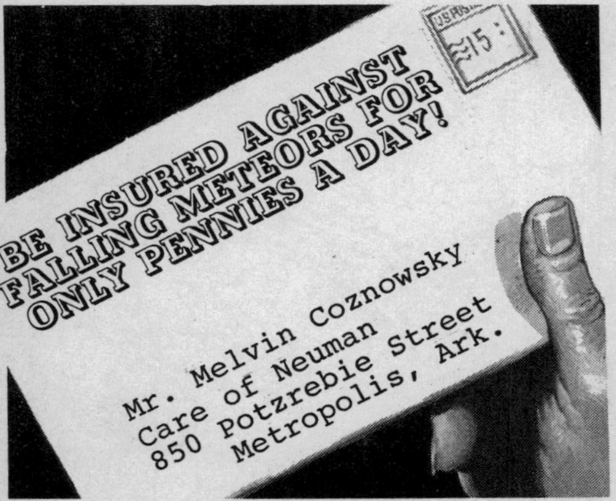
BE INSURED AGAINST FALLING METEORS FOR ONLY PENNIES A DAY!
Mr. Melvin Coznowsky
Care of Neuman
850 Potzrebie Street
Metropolis, Ark.

. . . because we never add up all those items that cost "only pennies a day" to see how their total cost can amount to thousands of dollars a year.

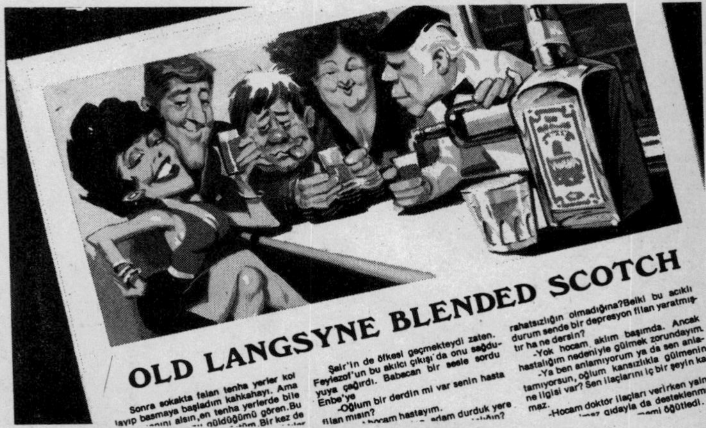
OLD LANGSYNE BLENDED SCOTCH

. . . because liquor companies always mention their product's mellow aging and smooth taste, but never warn us of the rotting liver and wild convulsions we can get from drinking it.

WE'LL ALWAYS BE SUCKERS FOR CLEVER ADVERTISING

...because every parent wants to believe that a $500 set of encyclopedias is all that's needed to transform his stupid kid into a Rhodes Scholar.

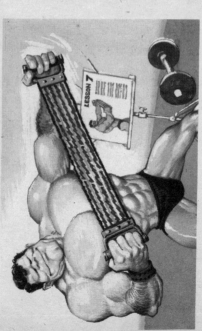

...because we mistakenly assume that the models pictured demonstrating "body-building equipment" were as scrawny as we are until they started using the stuff.

WE'LL ALWAYS BE SUCKERS FOR CLEVER ADVERTISING

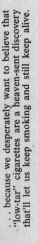

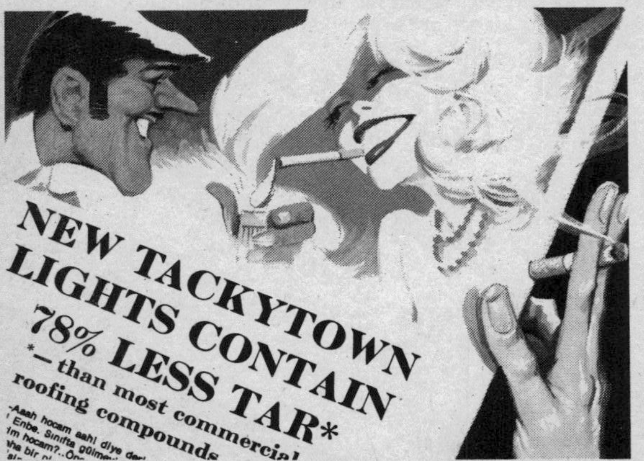
NEW TACKYTOWN
LIGHTS CONTAIN
78% LESS TAR*
*— than most commercia
roofing compounds

. . . because we desperately want to believe that "low-tar" cigarettes are a heaven-sent discovery that'll let us keep smoking and still keep alive.

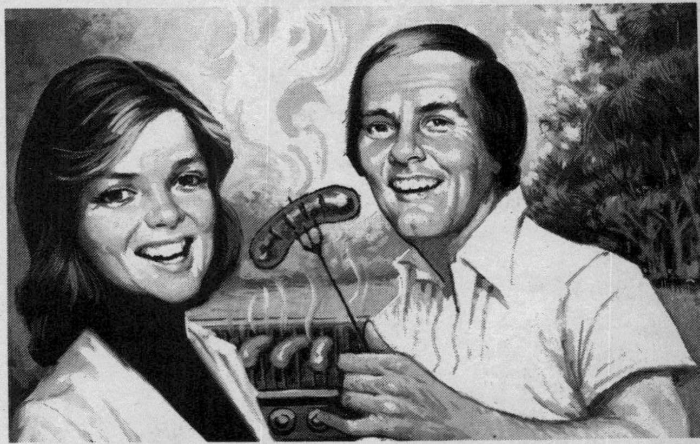

. . . because it boggles the minc to imagine a wonderful person like Pat Boone lying w ien he tells us that hot dogs are nutritious, even when they're not particularly.

WE'LL ALWAYS BE SUCKERS FOR CLEVER ADVERTISING

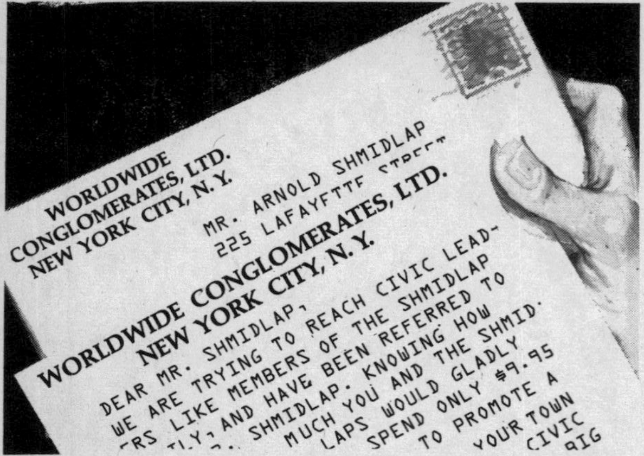

WORLDWIDE CONGLOMERATES, LTD.
NEW YORK CITY, N.Y.
MR. ARNOLD SHMIDLAP
225 LAFAYFTTE STREET
WORLDWIDE CONGLOMERATES, LTD.
NEW YORK CITY, N.Y.
DEAR MR. SHMIDLAP,
WE ARE TRYING TO REACH CIVIC LEAD-
ERS LIKE MEMBERS OF THE SHMIDLAP
AND HAVE BEEN REFERRED TO
SHMIDLAP. KNOWING HOW
MUCH YOU AND THE SHMID-
LAPS WOULD GLADLY
SPEND ONLY $9.95
TO PROMOTE A
YOUR TOWN
CIVIC

. . . because we're flattered when letters from big companies address us by our name, even though it's so obvious that they were written by a computer.

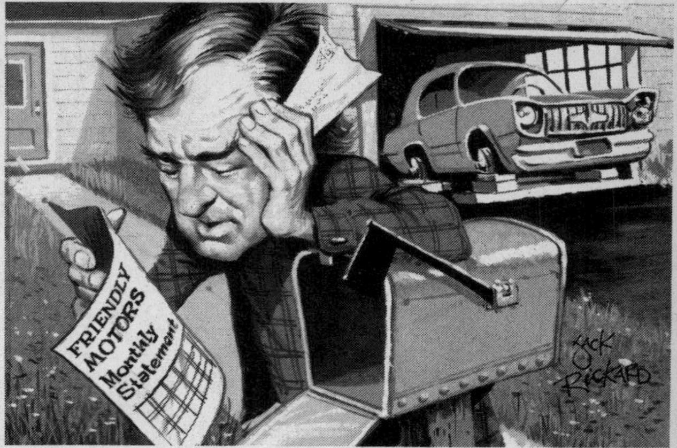

FRIENDLY MOTORS
Monthly Statement
JACK RICKARD

. . . because we lack the foresight to realize that 'easy monthly car payments' won't seem so easy when the car falls apart, and we're still paying for it.

WE GOT YOUR PENUMBRA DEPT.

Who Knows What Evils Lurk In The Hearts Of Men?

THE SHADOW KNOWS

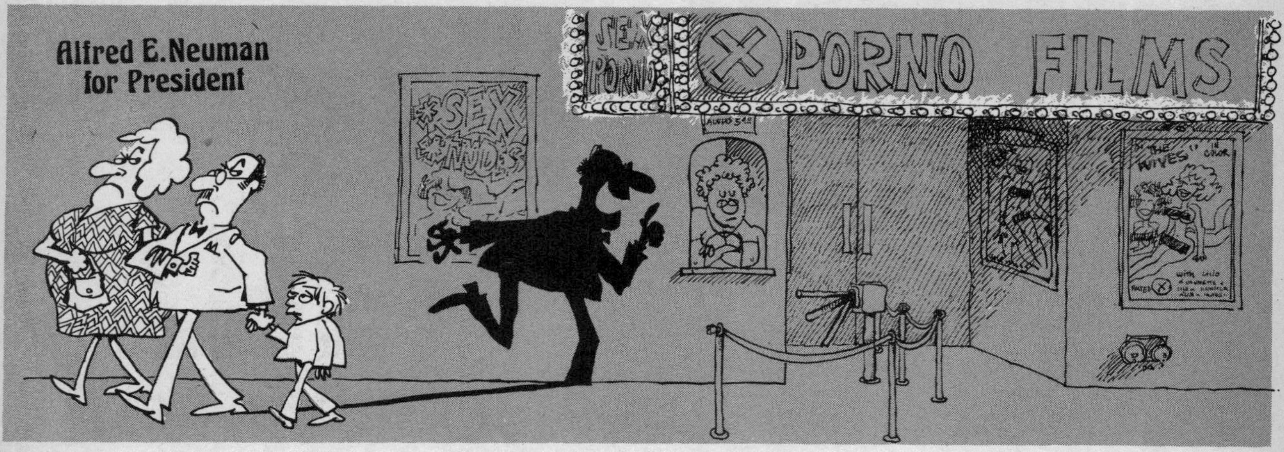
Alfred E. Neuman
for President
SEX
PORNO
PORNO FILMS
SEX
NUDES
"THE WIVES" IN COLOR
RATED X

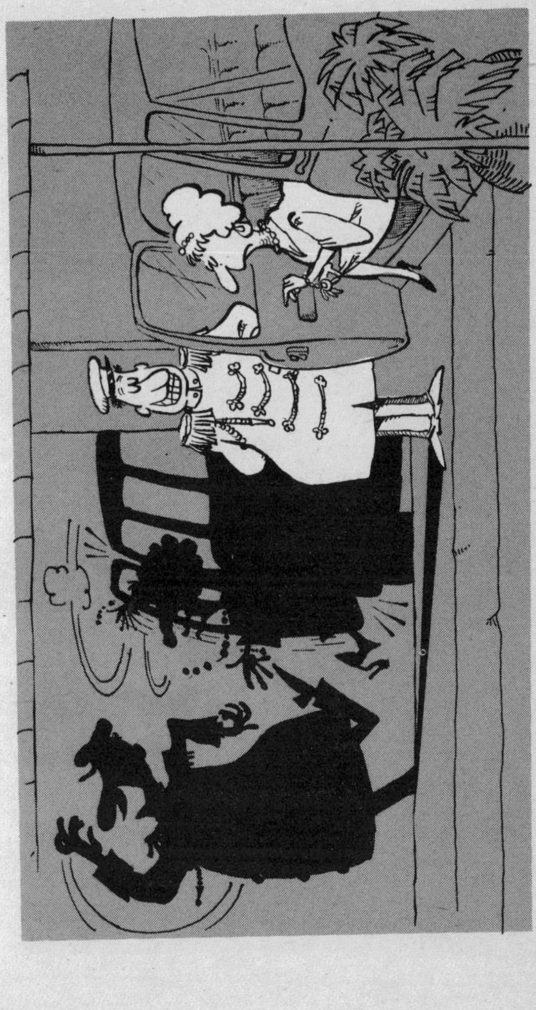

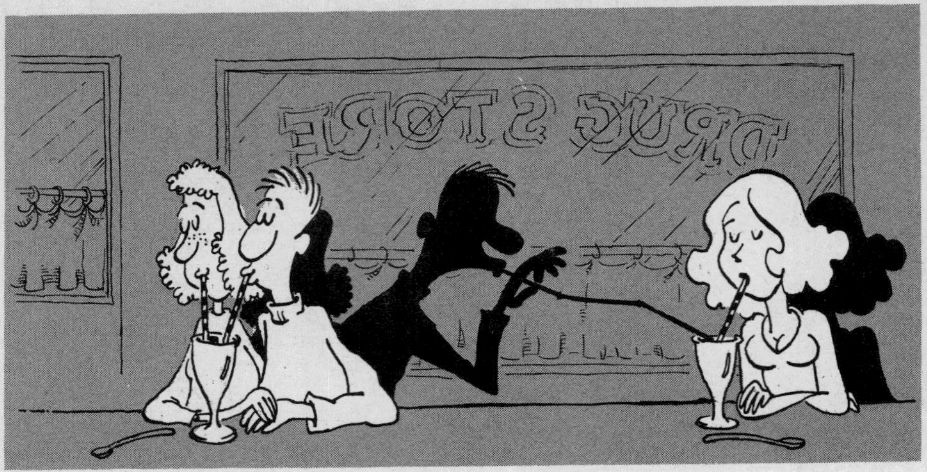
DRUG STORE

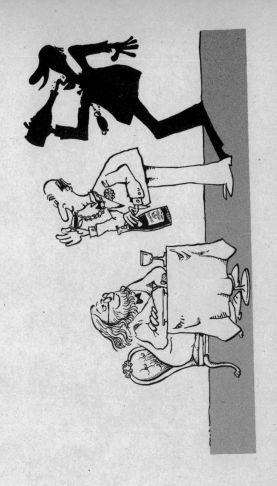

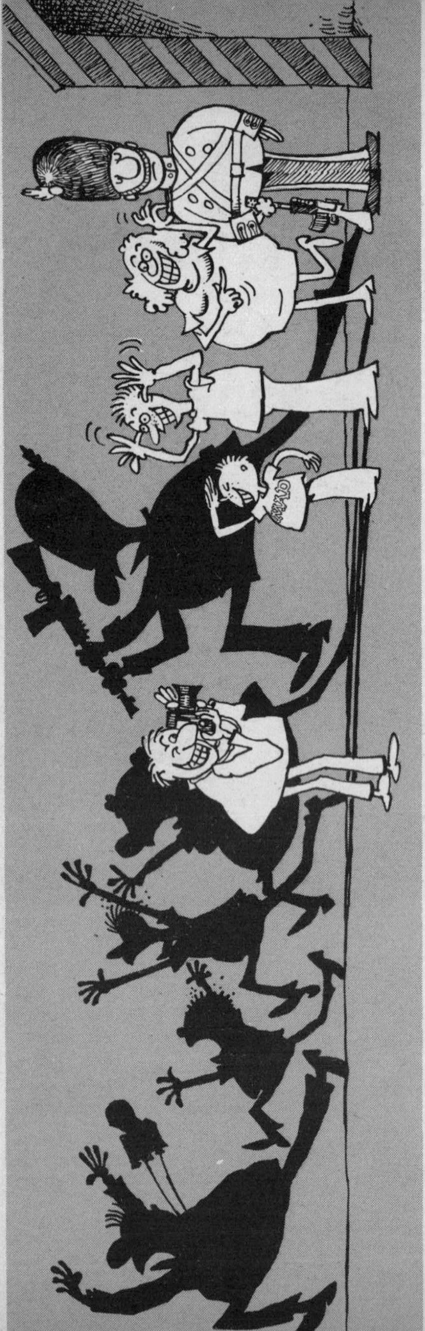

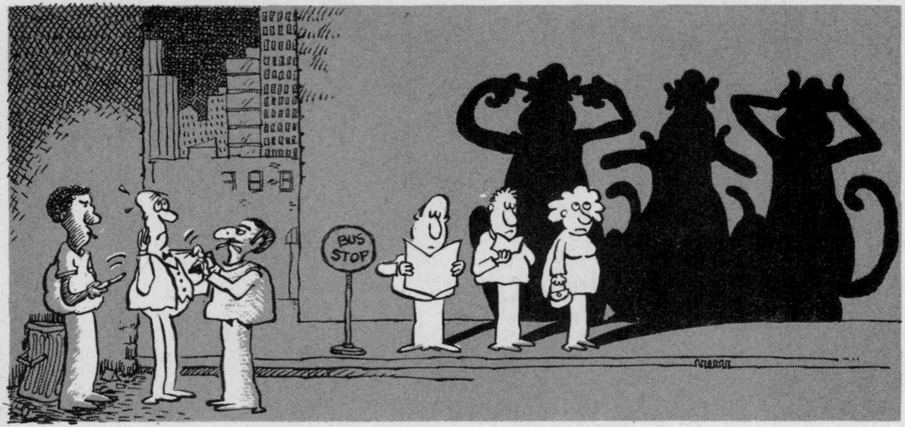
BUS STOP

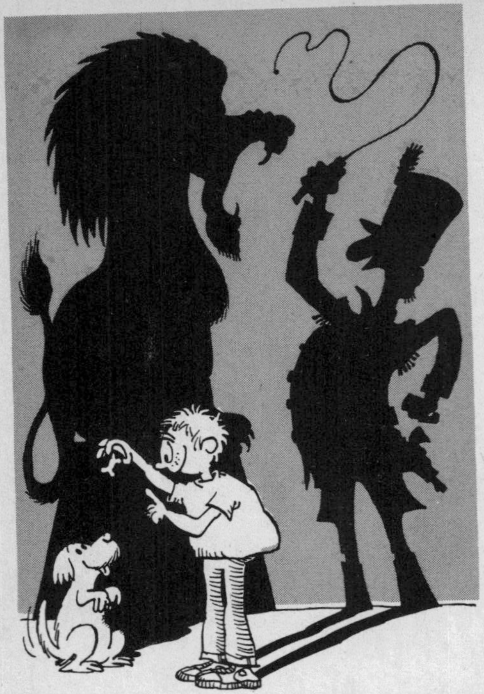

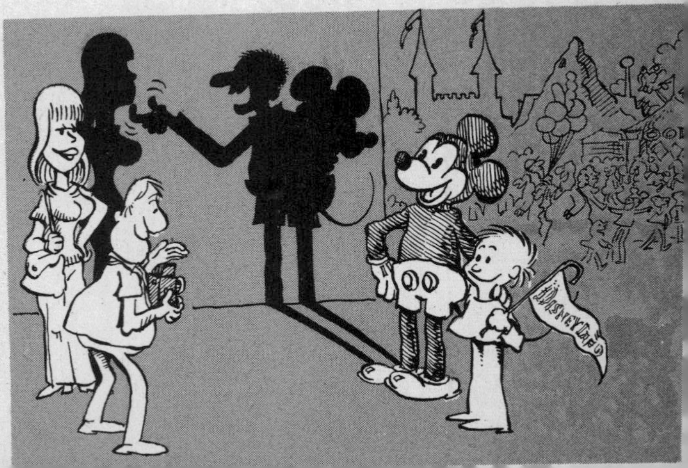
DISNEYLAND

MAD'S NEW PHOBIAS FOR THE '80'S

ARTIST: PAUL COKER   WRITER: JOHN FICARRA

SPLATAPHOBIA

Fear of learning that the plane you're about to board is a DC-10.

FRACASAPHOBIA

Fear of stopping by a strange bar and standing next to Billy Martin.

ROOTSAPHOBIA

Fear of having to be out of the house on the concluding night of a 7-part TV movie.

GACKAPHOBIA

Fear of catching your tie in your food processor.

OPECAPHOBIA

Fear of the price of gasoline going up while it's being pumped into your car.

CUTSEYPHOBIA

Fear of not being able to buy anything that doesn't have a "Peanuts" or "Sesame Street" character on it.

MEDIPHOBIA

Fear of checking out of a hospital even sicker than when you checked in.

BIMBOPHOBIA

Fear of being booked on a TV Talk Show between Cheryl Tiegs and Charo.

MALDENPHOBIA

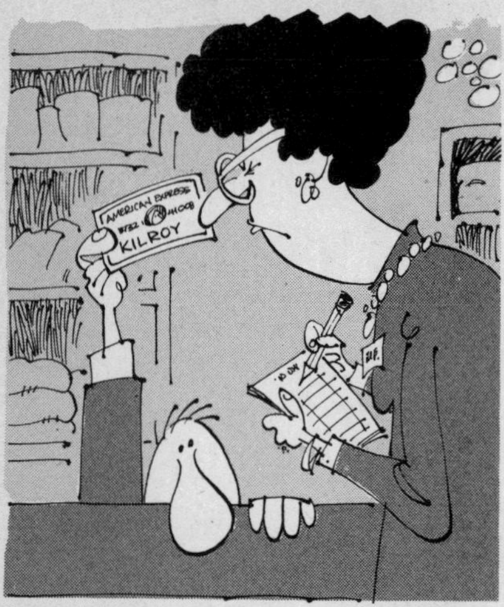
AMERICAN EXPRESS
KILROY

Fear of leaving home with your American Express Card and still not being recognized.

FELONIAPHOBIA

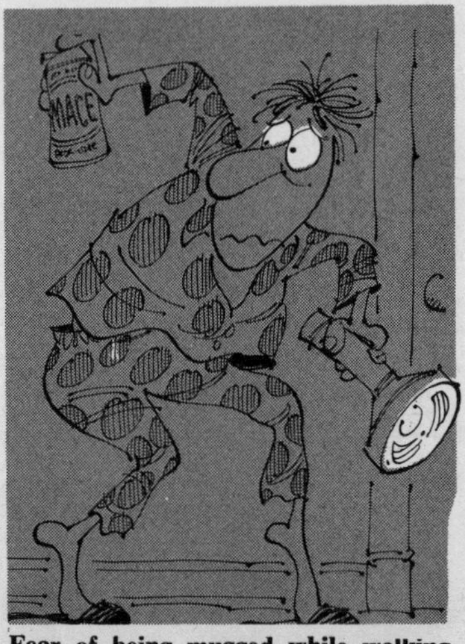
MACE

Fear of being mugged while walking from your bedroom to your bathroom.

DON MARTIN DEPT.

ONE BLAZING HOT DAY ON THE BEACH

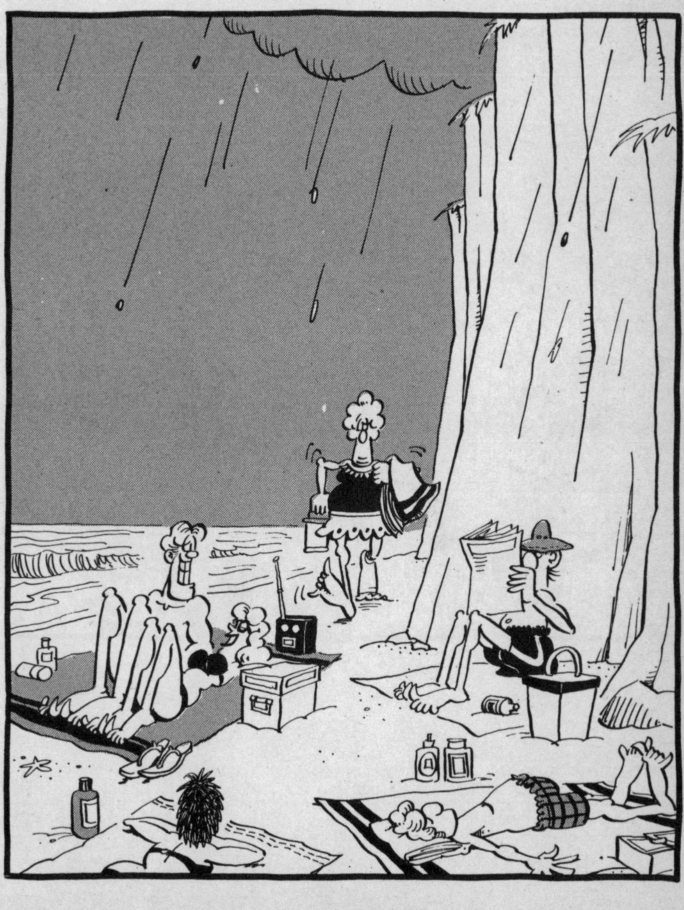

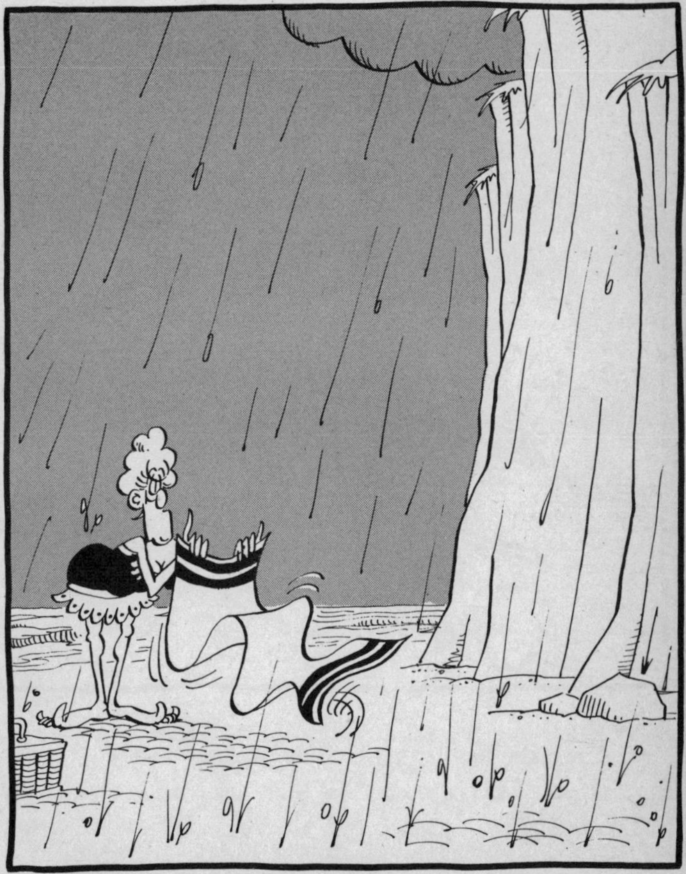

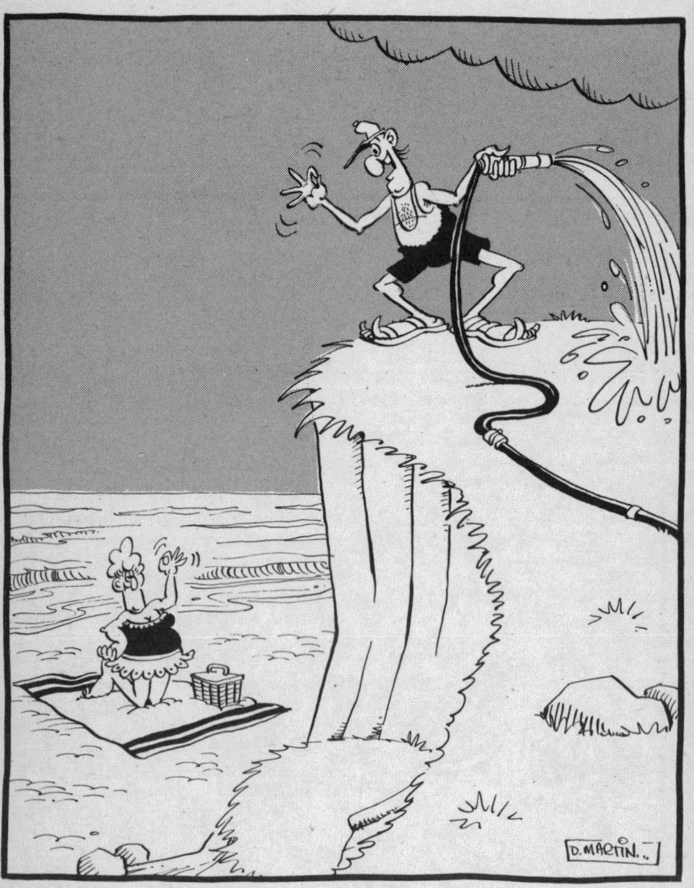
D. MARTIN

With more and more leisure time on our hands, and (thanks to inflation) less and less money to spend on hobbies and other activities to fill that time, here is—

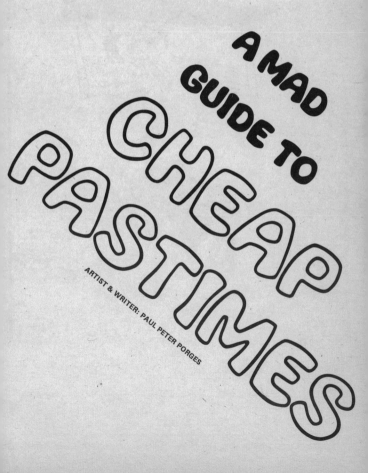

A MAD GUIDE TO CHEAP PASTIMES

ARTIST & WRITER: PAUL PETER PORGES

BODY-BUILDING BY
FURNITURE-PUMPING

TRAVEL SIGN-PAINTING

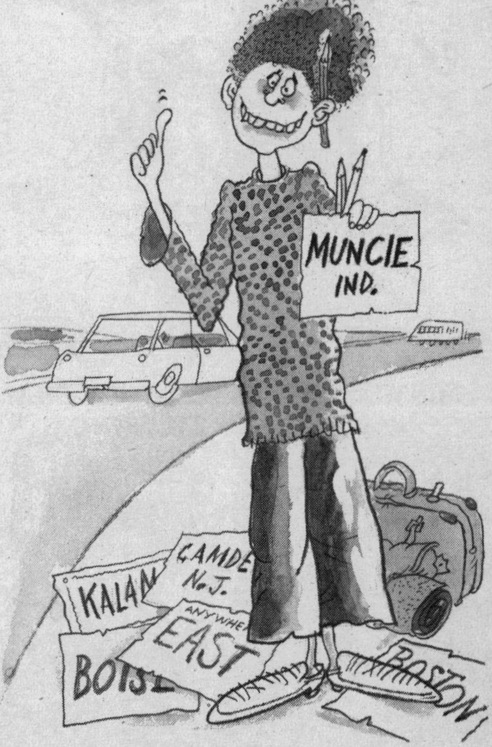
MUNCIE
IND.
CAMDE
N.J.
EAST
BOSTON

BEARD AND MOUSTACHE GROWING AND GROOMING

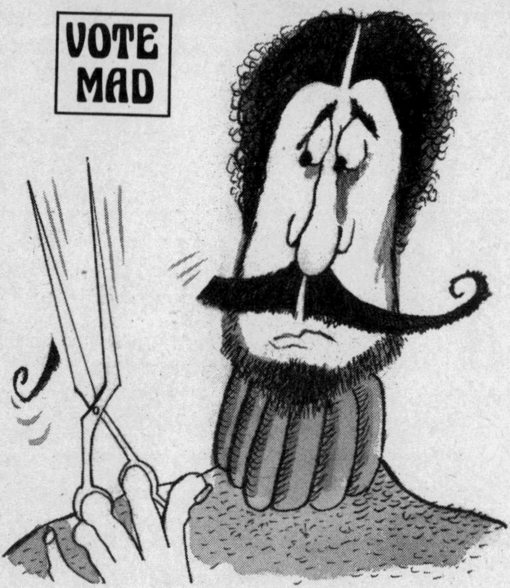
VOTE MAD

MINT-CONDITION FAST-FOOD-CHAIN PAPER NAPKIN-COLLECTING

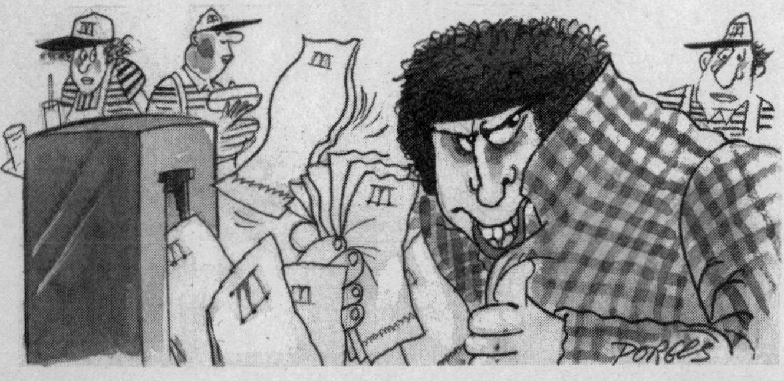
DORGES

TAP WATER-TASTING PARTIES

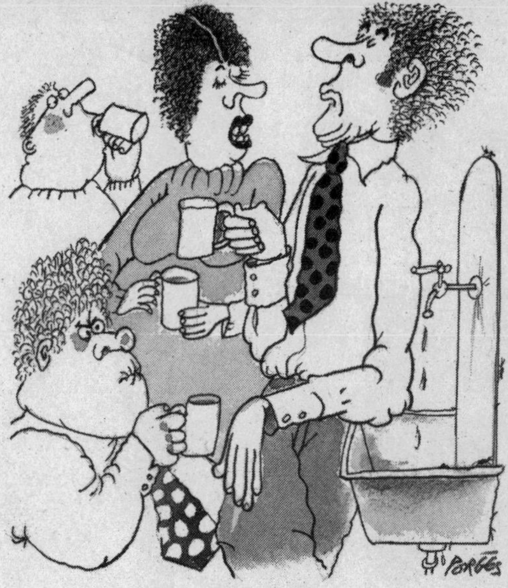

SUPERMARKET CART DRAG-RACING

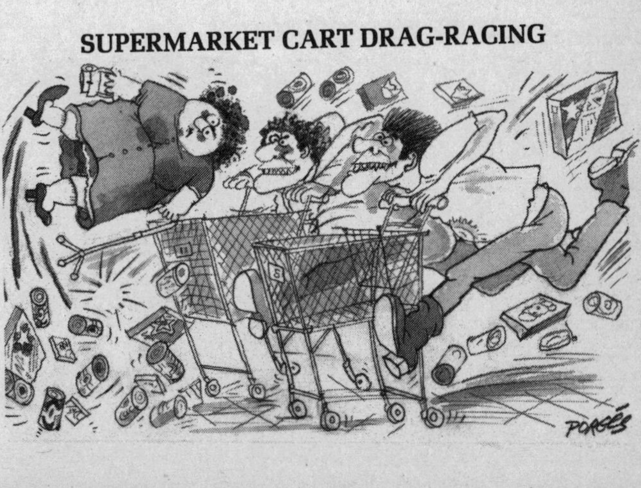

LOST COIN-FISHING

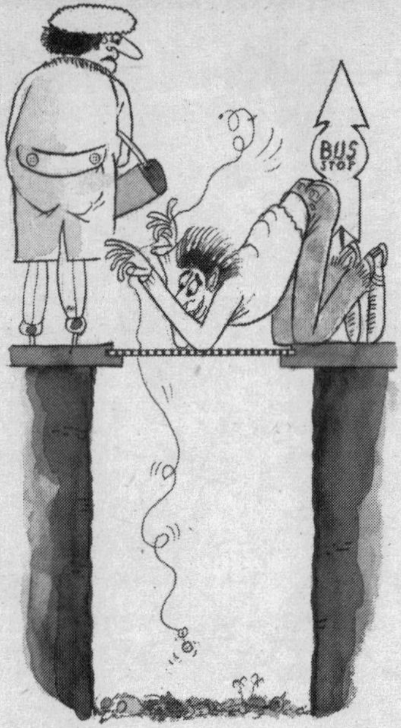
BUS
STOP

HOUSE FLY-COLLECTING

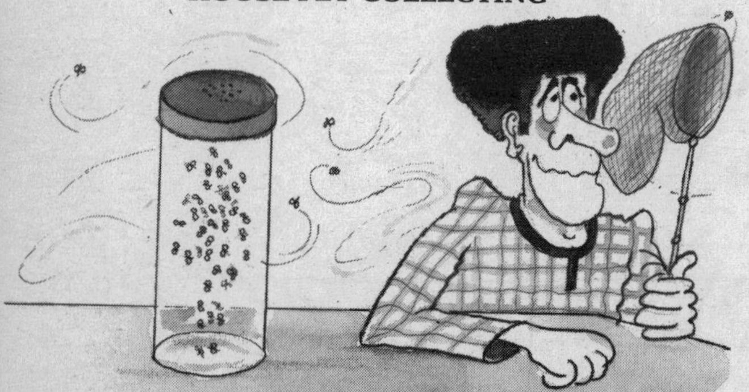

PAPERCLIP JEWELRY-MAKING

SMOG AND POLLUTION-WATCHING

USED PAPERWARE-RESTORING

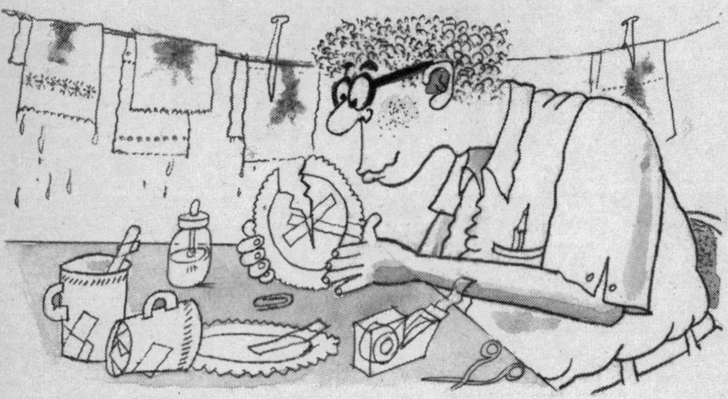

CRATES-INTO-FURNITURE-MAKING

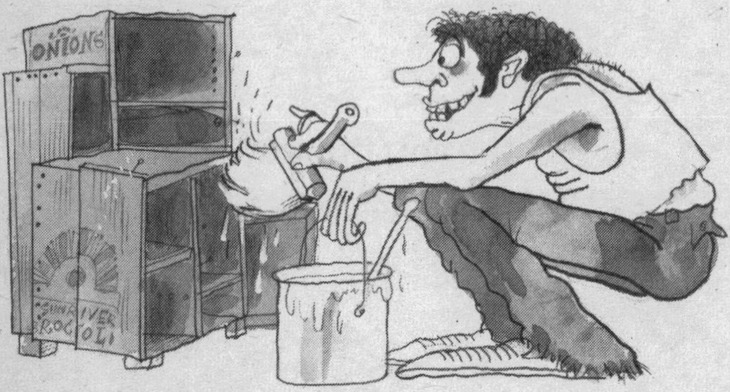
ONIONS

KITCHENWARE TIMPANI-PLAYING

NOSE BOOGER-DIGGING-AND-ROLLING

★ ★ ★ ★ ★ ★ ★ ★
★ **Alfred E.** ★
★ **Neuman** ★
★ **for** ★
★ **President** ★
★ ★ ★ ★ ★ ★ ★ ★

KARATE CAR-ANTIQUEING

SIDEWALK CAFE-WATCHING

DON MARTING DEPT.

LATE ONE AFTERNOON ON AN INTERSTATE HIGHWAY

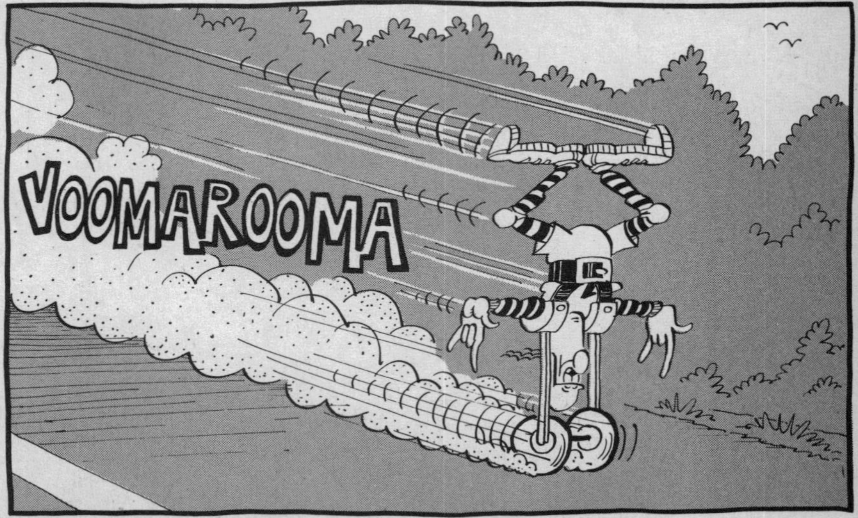
VOOMAROOMA

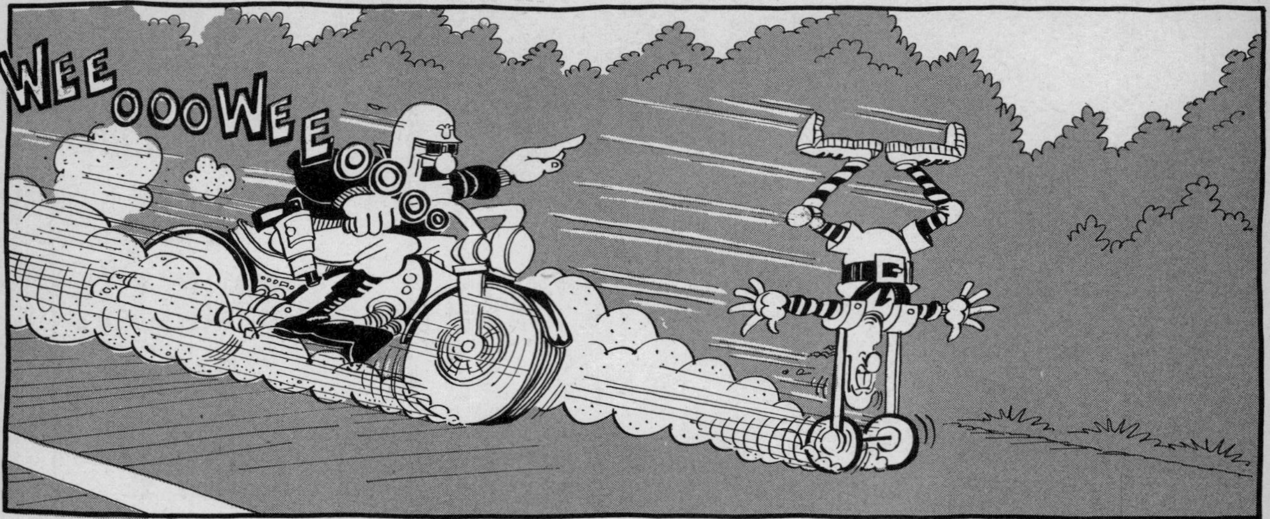
WEEOOOWEEOOOOO

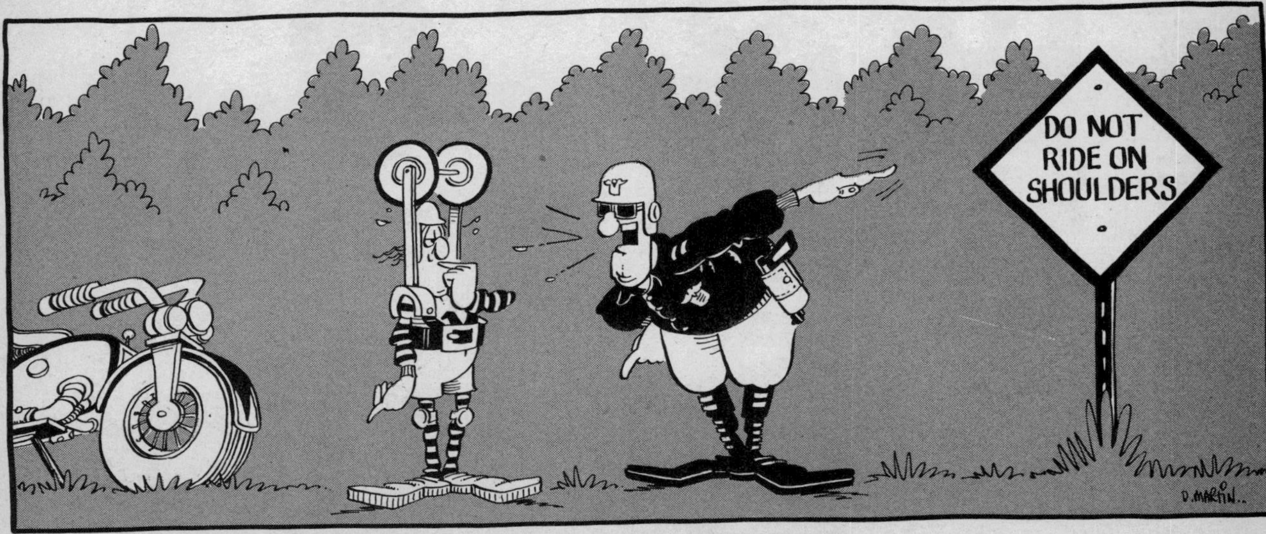
DO NOT RIDE ON SHOULDERS
D. MARTIN

INSIDE POOP DEPT.

A MAD LOOK AT SOME...

CELEB DIAPERS

ARTIST: BOB CLARKE WRITER: PAUL PETER PORGES

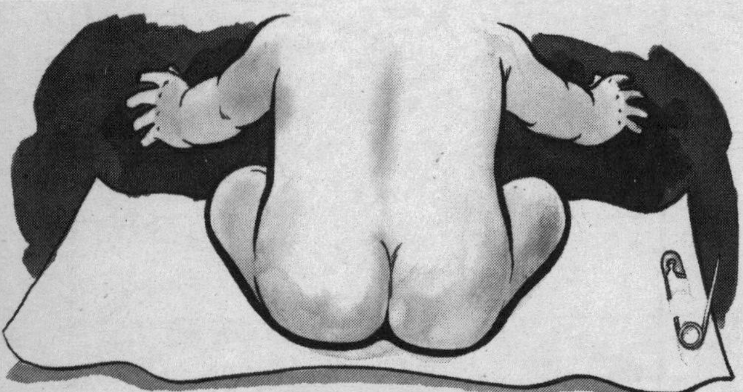

LADY GODIVA

RITIES

**REMEMBER!
THIS WAS
BEFORE
"PAMPERS"!**

PYTHAGORAS

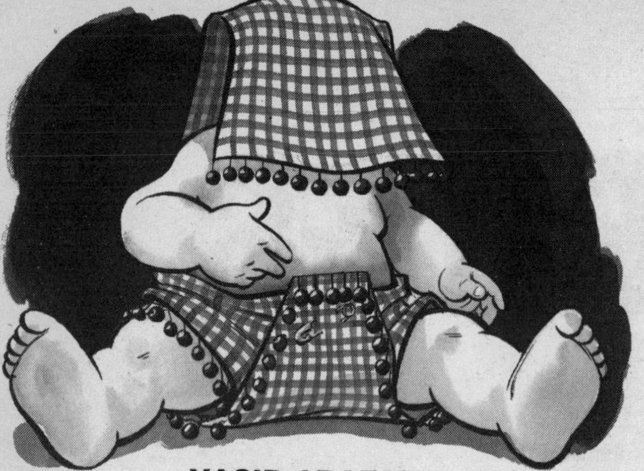

YASIR ARAFAT

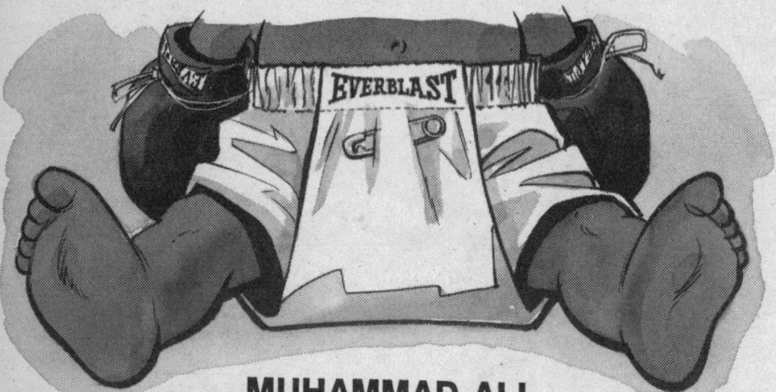
EVERBLAST

MUHAMMAD ALI

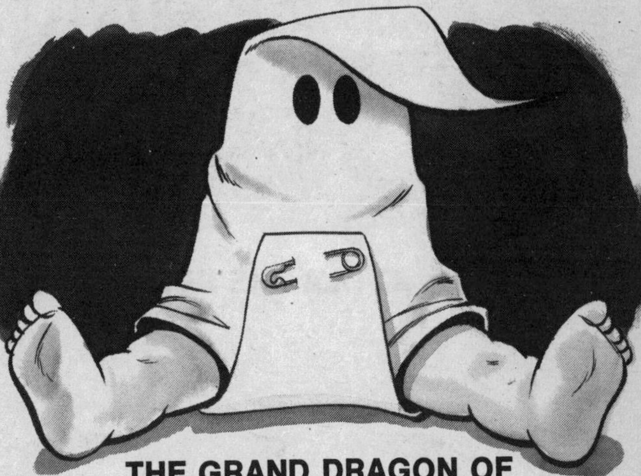

THE GRAND DRAGON OF
THE KU KLUX KLAN

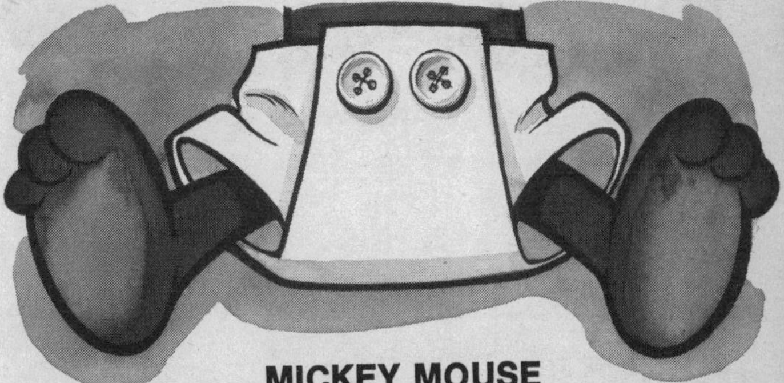

MICKEY MOUSE

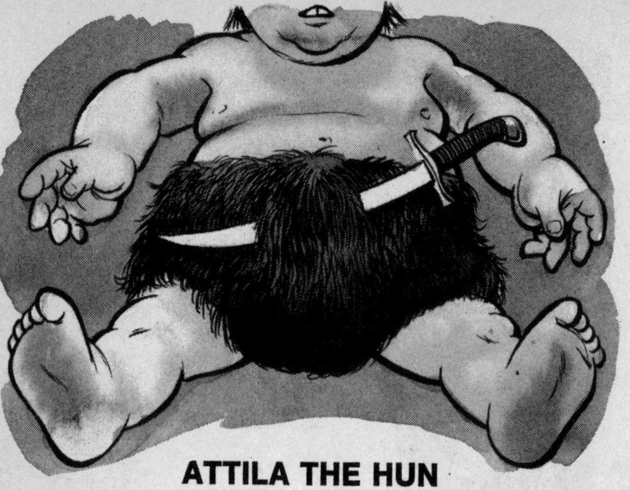

ATTILA THE HUN

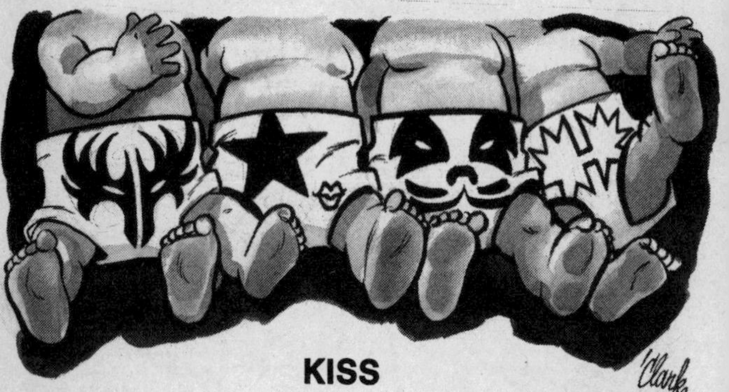
Clarke

KISS

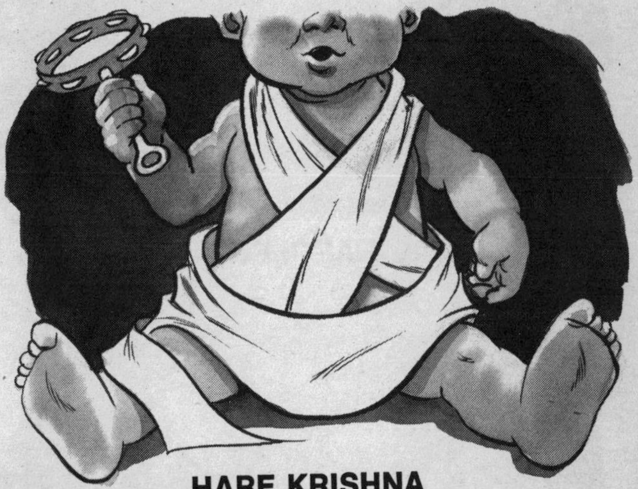

HARE KRISHNA

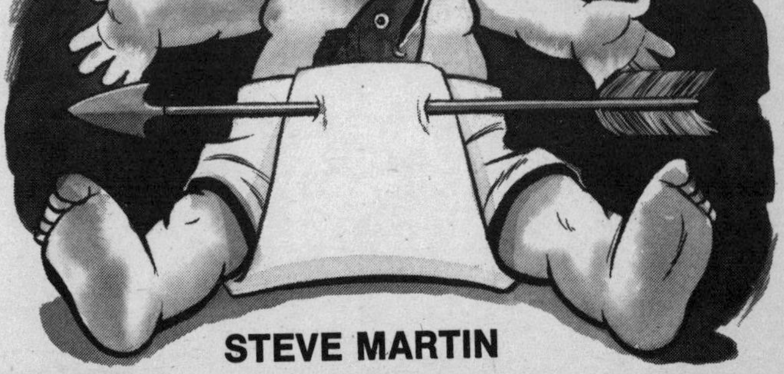

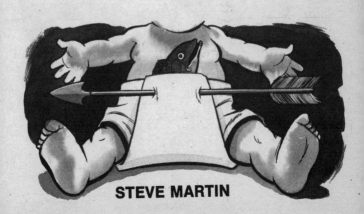

STEVE MARTIN

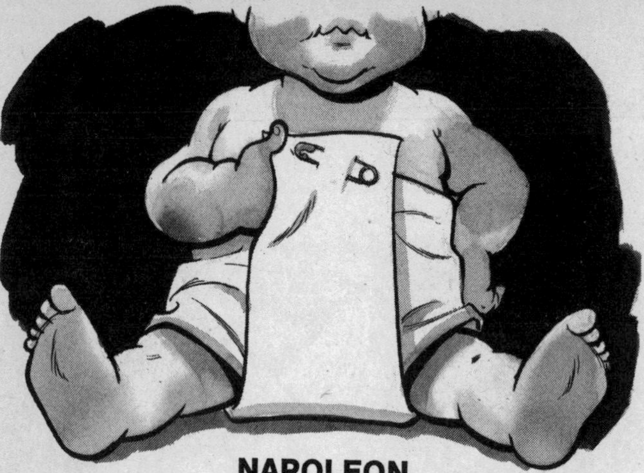

NAPOLEON

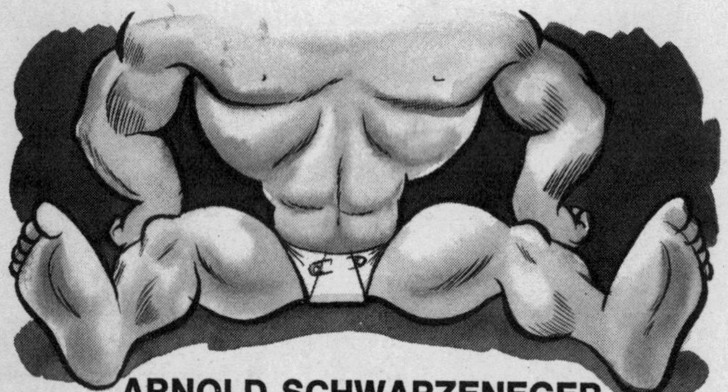

ARNOLD SCHWARZENEGER

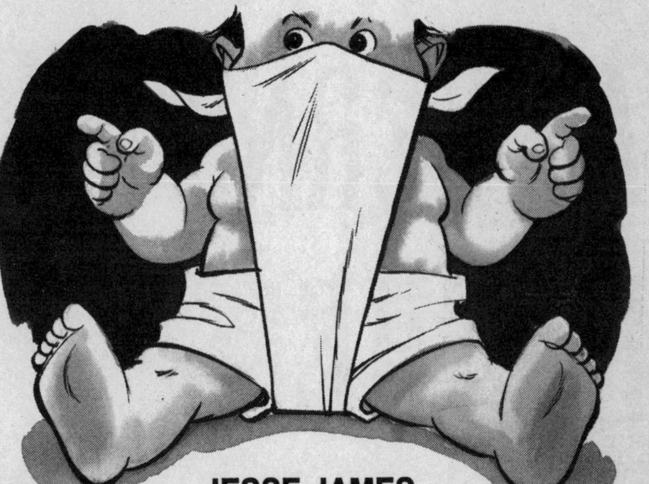

JESSE JAMES

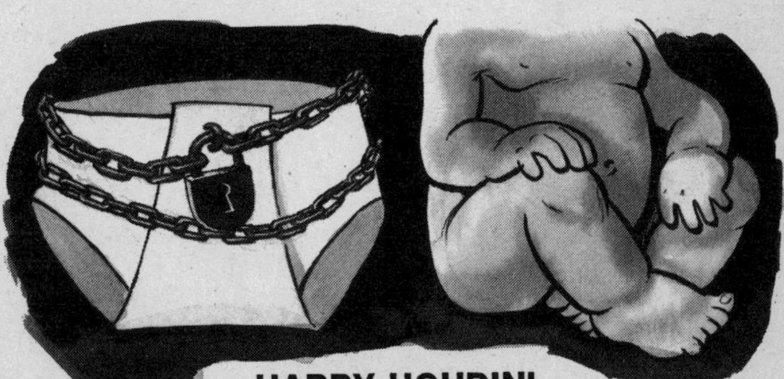

HARRY HOUDINI

ONE AFTERNOON IN THE FAR EAST

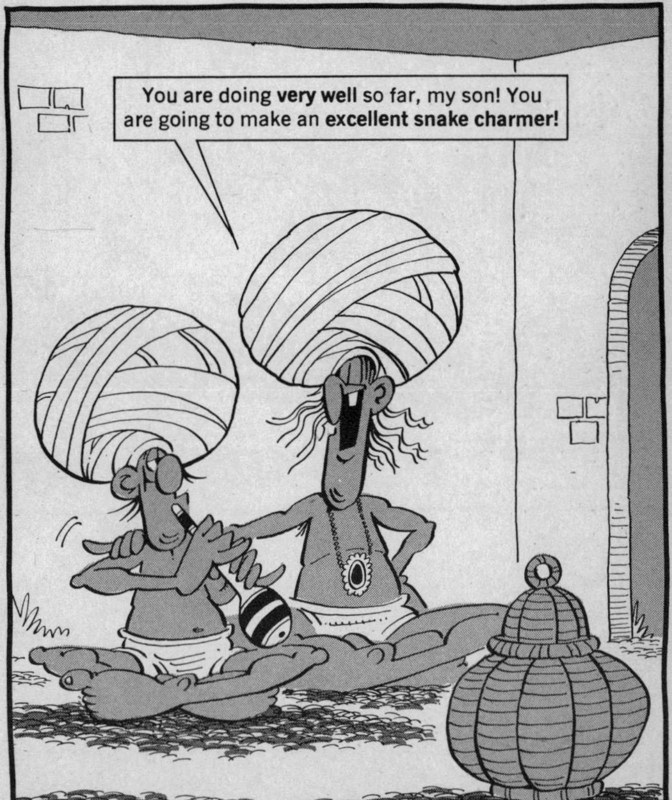
You are doing **very well** so far, my son! You are going to make an **excellent snake charmer!**

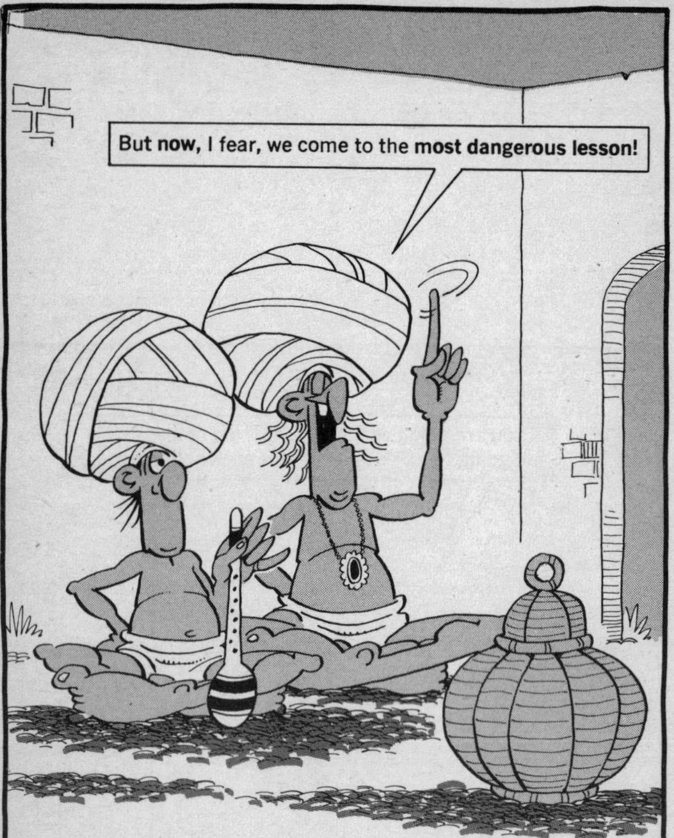
But now, I fear, we come to the most dangerous lesson!

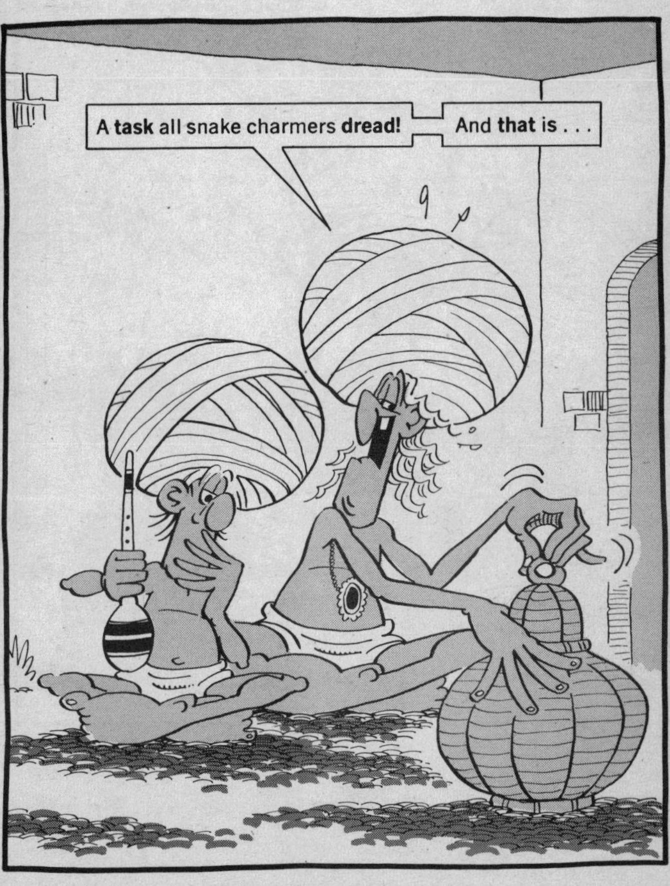
A task all snake charmers dread!
And that is . . .

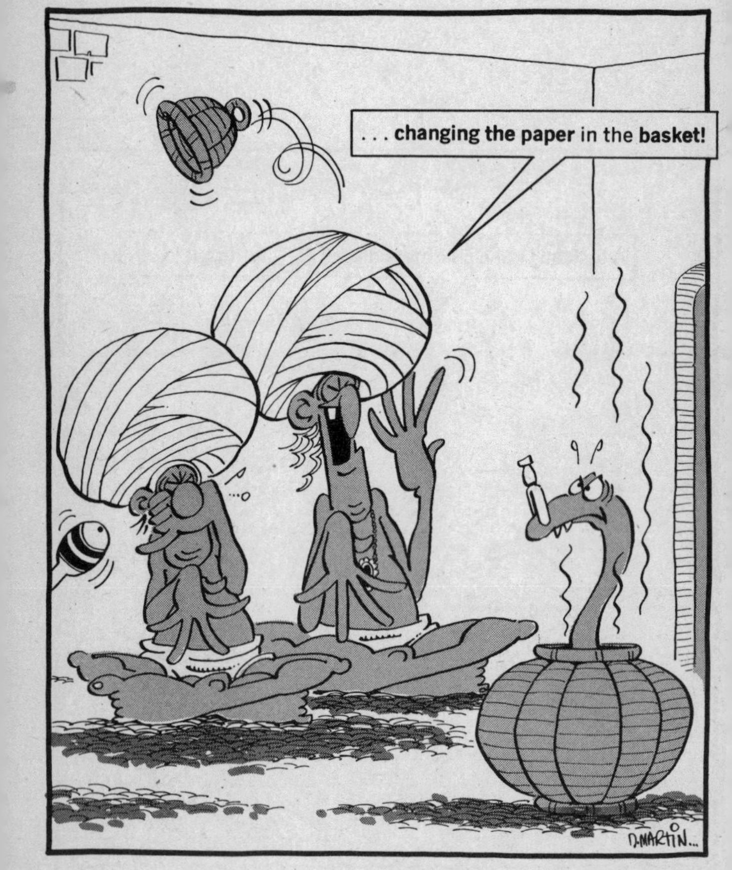
. . . changing the paper in the basket!
D.MARTIN...

Since a complete set of Criminal Law books would fill one whole room in a library, it's hard to believe that most of the outrageous things done to us by other people have not as yet been ruled illegal. Obviously, these statutes need a complete overhaul to provide punishment for the hordes of self-centered idiots who theaten our safety and sanity. MAD is already lobbying for such legislation, and it's only a matter of time before we'll be able to call the Police to arrest clods who commit:

EVERYDAY CRIMES THAT SHOULD BE PUNISHED

ARTIST: HARRY NORTH, ESQ.   **WRITER: TOM KOCH**

Felonious Throat Hawking

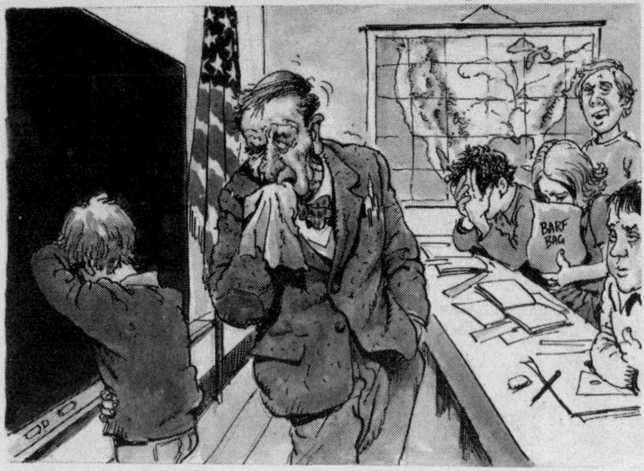
BARF BAG

This abominable infraction is also known as snorting, glonking, deep snuffling, bronchial rattling and early morning phlegm raising. It is most often committed by elderly school teachers who thoughtlessly try to dispel their mucous as they simultaneously disgust their students. In order to stamp out this nauseating crime in our lifetime, convicted throat hawkers shall henceforth be led to a public place and forced to eat luke warm raw oysters while standing barefoot in a bucket of worms.

Petty Parking Space Grabbing

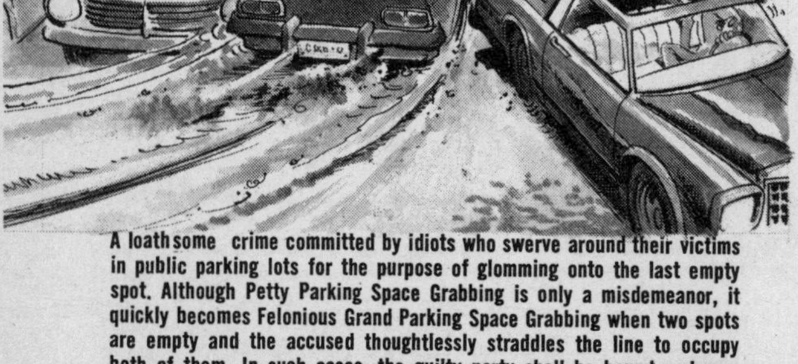

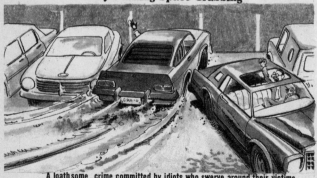

A loathsome crime committed by idiots who swerve around their victims in public parking lots for the purpose of glomming onto the last empty spot. Although Petty Parking Space Grabbing is only a misdemeanor, it quickly becomes Felonious Grand Parking Space Grabbing when two spots are empty and the accused thoughtlessly straddles the line to occupy both of them. In such cases, the guilty party shall be bound and gagged and rolled into the main aisle of public parking facility, where he will be at the mercy of enraged little old ladies driving Ramblers.

Cruel And Inhuman Pants Manufacturing

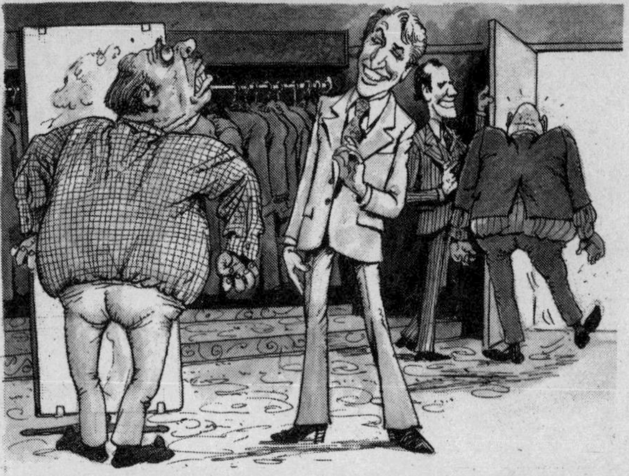

The crime committed by unscrupulous clothing manufacturers who eliminate several square feet of necessary material from every pair of pants they make. In promoting this torturous style, said manufacturers are deemed responsible for the epidemic of Groin Cramp and Crotch Agony that have seized the male population. Guilty individuals apprehended and convicted shall be forced to serve long terms in solitary confinement wearing jockey shorts originally designed for Herve Villechaize.

Aggravated Motorcycle Vrooming

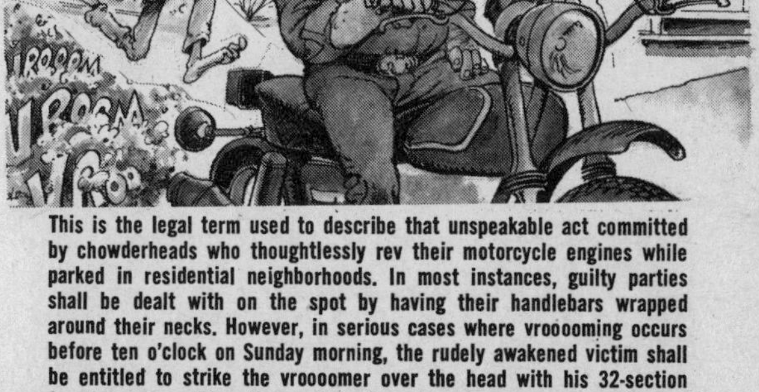

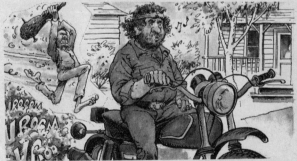

This is the legal term used to describe that unspeakable act committed by chowderheads who thoughtlessly rev their motorcycle engines while parked in residential neighborhoods. In most instances, guilty parties shall be dealt with on the spot by having their handlebars wrapped around their necks. However, in serious cases where vrooooming occurs before ten o'clock on Sunday morning, the rudely awakened victim shall be entitled to strike the vroooomer over the head with his 32-section Sunday paper until major skull fracture has been righteously inflicted.

Gross Negligence Of Civil Foot Wiping

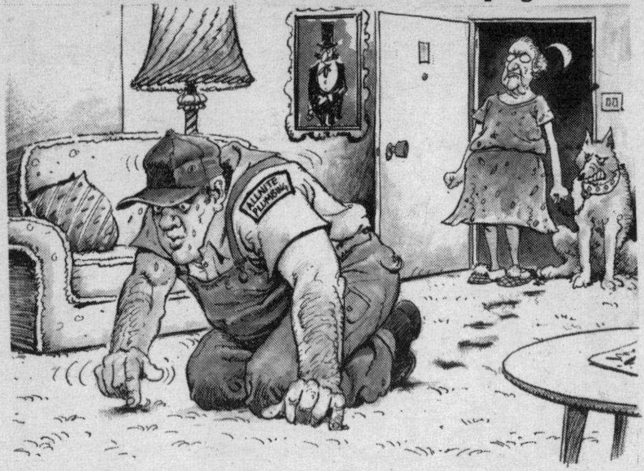
ALLNITE PLUMBING

A disgusting act that makes any slob liable to arrest when apprehended clomping across the victim's pastel carpet while wearing unwiped shoes tainted with axle grease, doggy-doo, chewing gum and/or squashed garbage. The convicted tracker-inner shall be required to atone for his slovenly actions by impersonating a throw rug and covering the stain with his body until Rug Cleaners can be called in to undo the damage.

Illegal Grope And Seizure

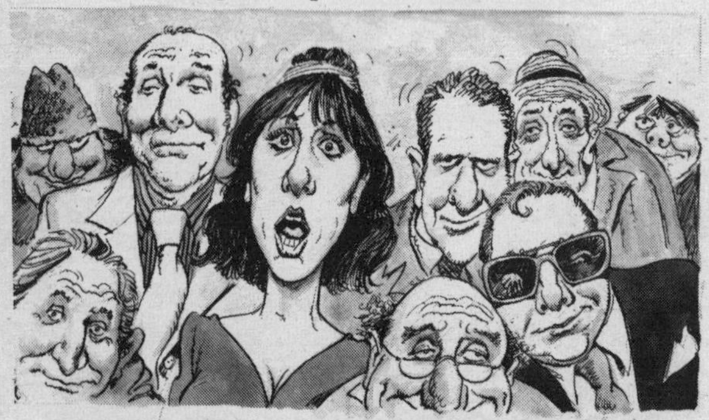

This form of sneaky activity is made indictable to protect members of the feminine gender who prefer not to be groped or seized while attending such events as football games, parades and rush hour bus boardings. Members of the masculine gender judged guilty of premeditated groping shall be dunked, seat first, into a lobster tank, and required to suffer the pain and humiliation of having their posteriors pinched for a term of not more than three hours, nor less than one hour per offense.

Malicious Shpritzing

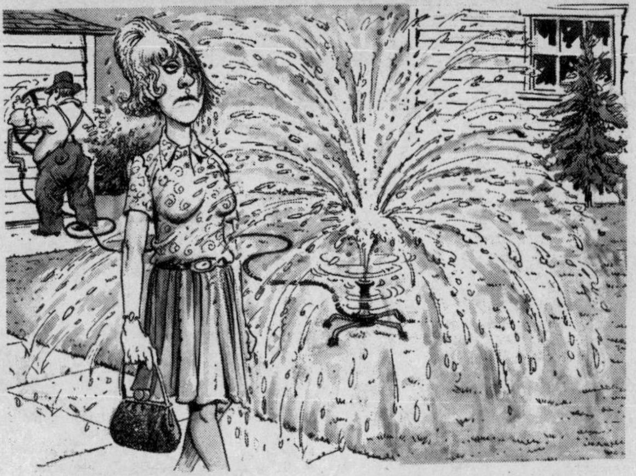

The high crime committed by clods who deliberately install their lawn sprinklers in such a way that no pedestrian can pass their house without suffering drenched feet and ankles. A first offender convicted of this crime shall be required to stand at attention in his front yard through one entire cloudburst. For the two-time loser, the punishment shall be increased to total permanent drowning by means of hurricane.

Bureaucratic Behavior With Pompous Intent

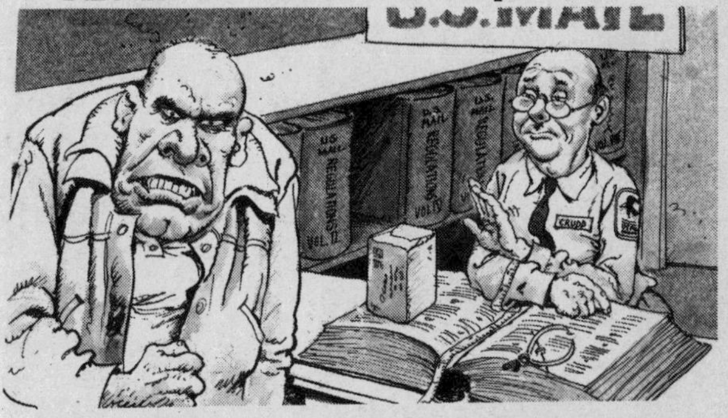
CRUDD

This violation of the Criminal Code is committed by Postal Clerks who invariably feel compelled to drag out a big volume of government regulations to find some new reason for rejecting every package presented for mailing. Public servants who display this form of arrogance shall be painfully incarcerated in a corner collection box until the next mail pick-up, which is usually scheduled to occur late that afternoon but often fails to take place until some time the following Wednesday.

Compound Check-Out Counter Stalling

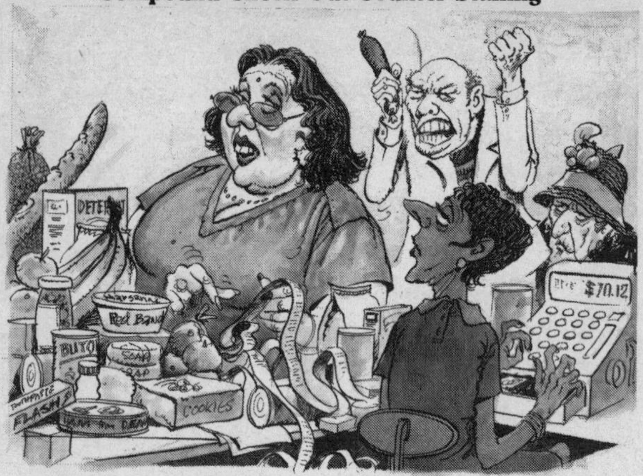
$70.12
COOKIES
FLASH
Red Band

This felony is chargeable against any person ahead of you on a Supermarket check-out line who engages in the following indecent acts: (1) Arguing with the checker over each blurred price marking; (2) comparing register tapes against all items purchased; or (3) attempting to cash a check without presenting any form of identification. All those ajudged guilty of said crimes shall be required to spend the rest of their natural lives pushing shopping carts with broken, stuck wheels.

Premature Elevator Button Pushing

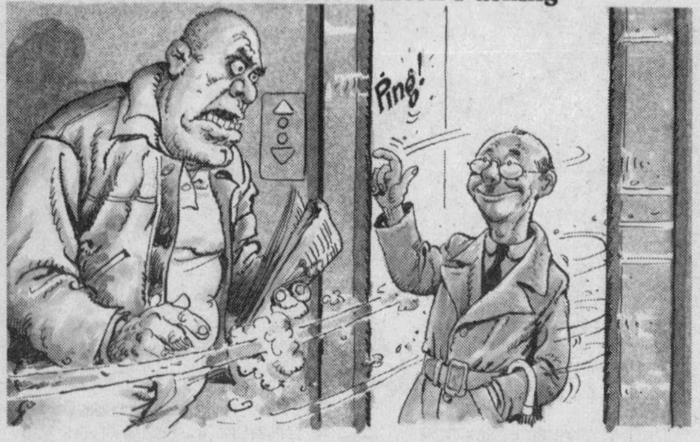
Ping!

The inhuman offense perpetrated by cretins who rush ahead to board the elevator you've been waiting for, and then immediately punch a button that causes the door to close before you can get on. A victim of such barbarous behavior shall be allowed to retaliate by throwing the main switch, thereby trapping the wrongdoer between floors until he is driven stark staring mad by either claustrophobia, or that sickening Muzak.

Conspiracy To Reveal Movie Plots

A serious infraction chargeable against any movie goer who has seen a picture before and insists on revealing the suspenseful details in a loud voice that you can't help overhearing. This crime shall be punished by chaining the perpetrator to his theater seat for an entire Nelson Eddy—Jeanette MacDonald Film Festival . . . after which, he must remain awake long enough to describe the plot of each picture in detail.

Drunken Telephone Dialing

The act of operating a telephone while under the influence of alcohol is a felony when committed between midnight and dawn by those who dial the numbers of innocent strangers in a fumbling attempt to reach old army buddies, long lost girlfriends, etc. Persons convicted shall be forced to spend 90 days answering irate phone calls that come into the complaint department of a notoriously shoddy Television Repair Service.

Impatient Honking In The First Degree

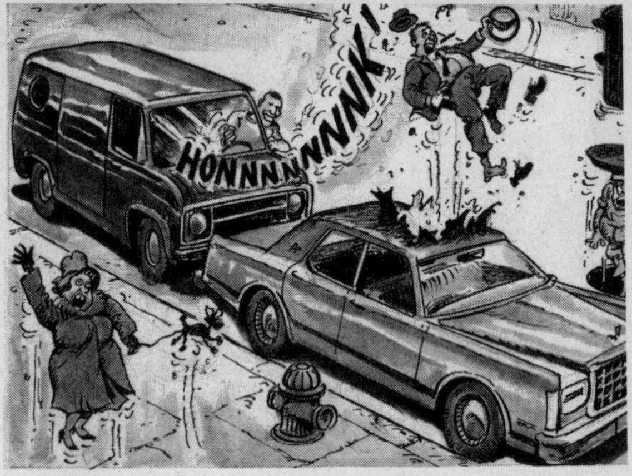
HONNNNNNNNNNK!

Chargeable against the creep in the car behind you who feels he must display his superior reflexes, the instant a traffic light turns green, by pressing his horn button faster than you can depress your accelerator pedal. Any perpetrator of this atrocity shall be mercilessly made to endure a lifetime of being awakened each morning by an alarm clock whose bell has been replaced with an ear-splitting diesel truck horn.

Forced Nuzzling With Accompanying Bad Breath

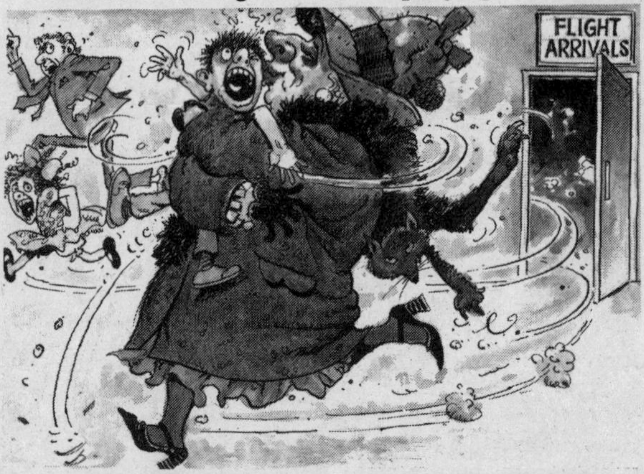
FLIGHT
ARRIVALS

A form of unacceptable behavior that violates the civil rights and the nasal passages of defenseless minors with unwanted hugging of distant relatives. Harshest punishment shall be reserved for aunts with large bosoms and cheap dentures who have the potential to suffocate children as well as nauseate them. In such cases, the convicted criminal shall be imprisoned up to one full year—in a zoo cage with an affectionate polar bear who always eats raw fish and never brushes after every meal.

DON MARTIN DEPT.

LATE ONE NIGHT IN A BANK

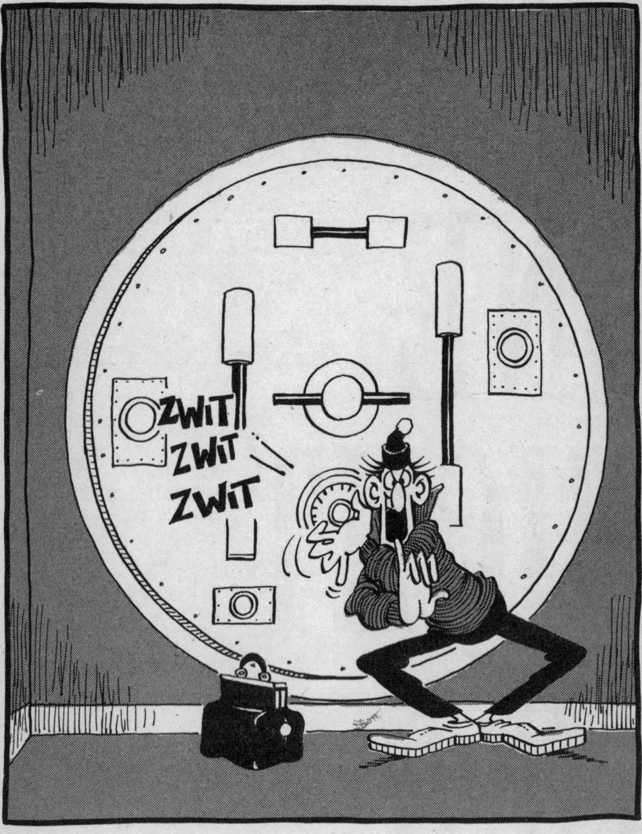
ZWIT
ZWIT
ZWIT

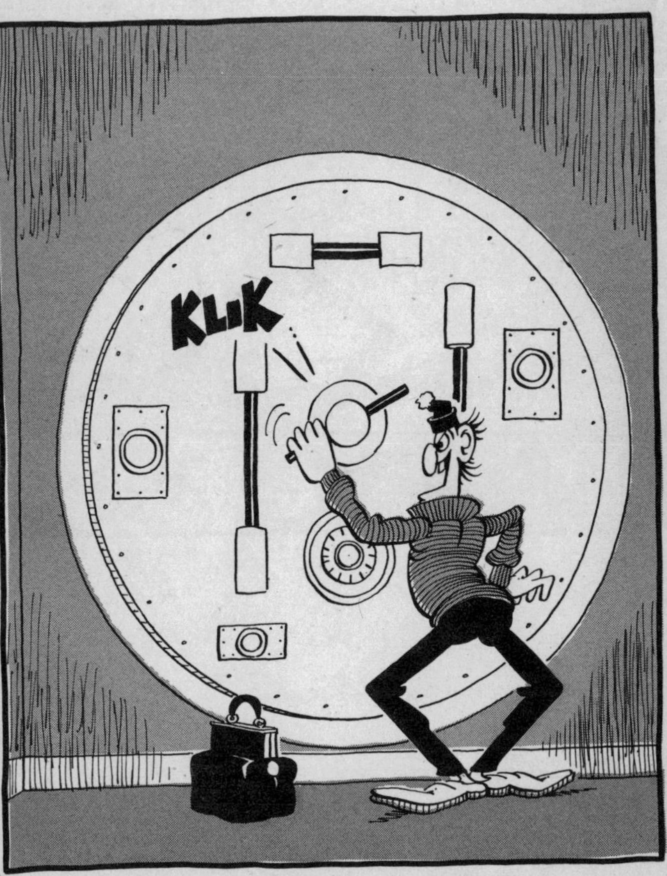
KLIK

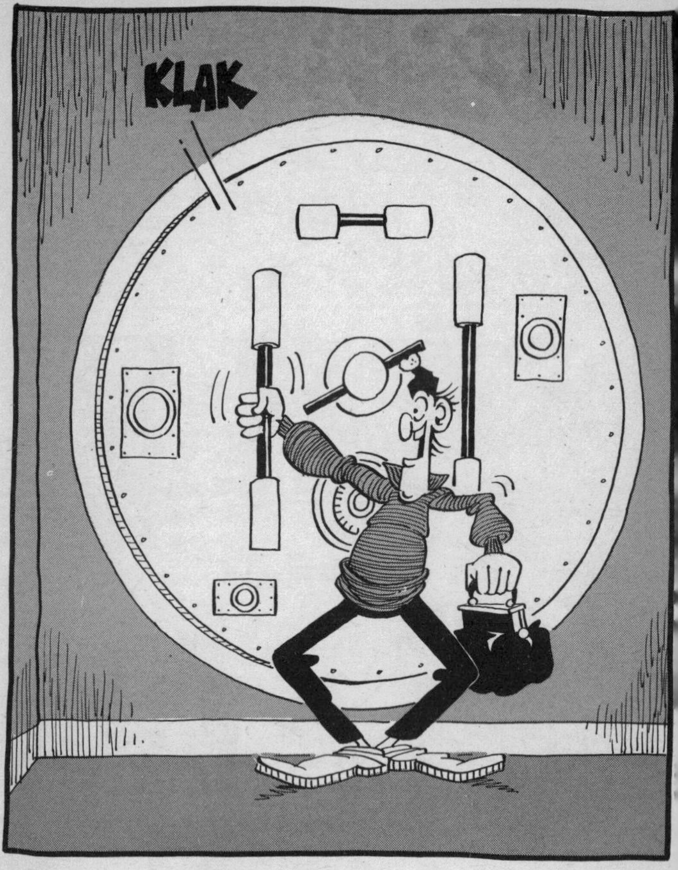
KLAK

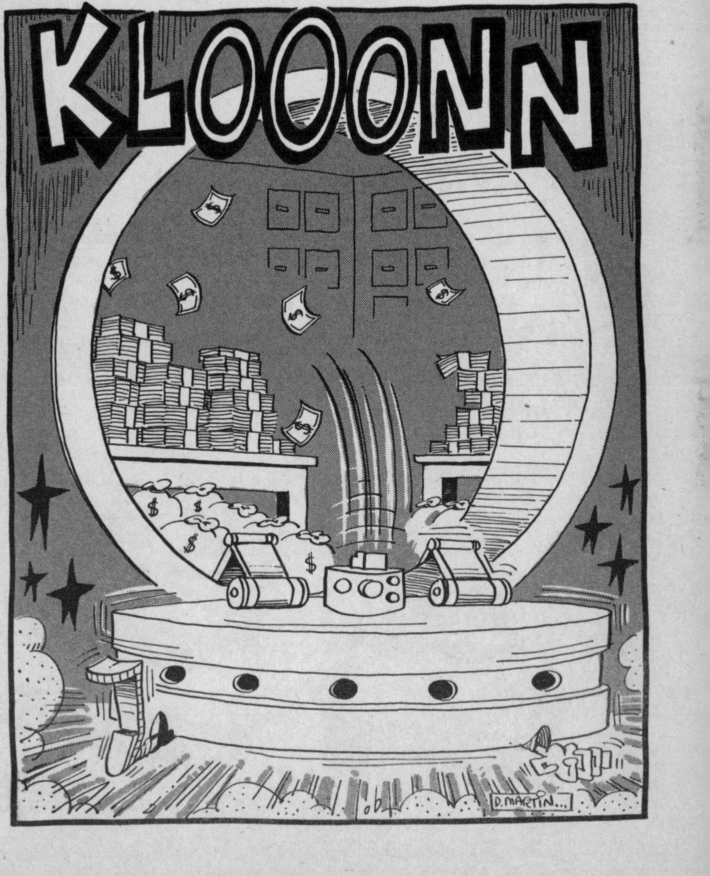
KLOOONN
D.MARTIN...

BERG's-EYE VIEW DEPT.

THE LI

SIDE

PARKING

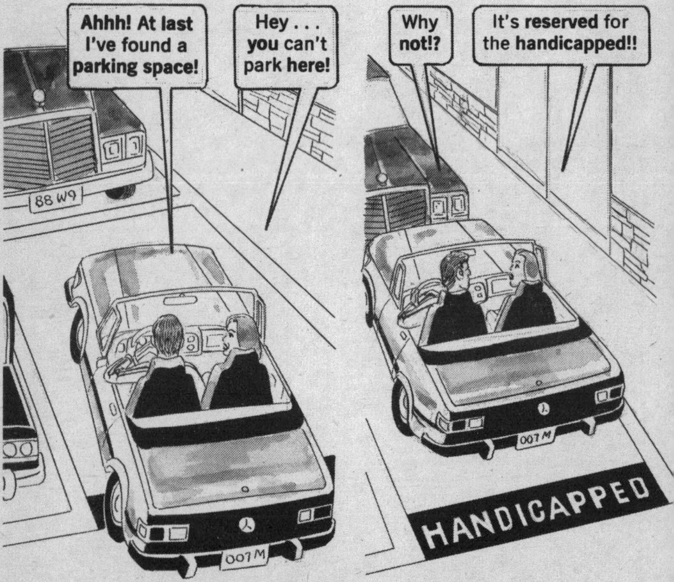
Ahhh! At last I've found a parking space!
Hey . . . you can't park here!
88 W9
007 M
Why not!?
It's reserved for the handicapped!!
007 M
HANDICAPPED

GHTER OF...

ARTIST & WRITER:
DAVE BERG

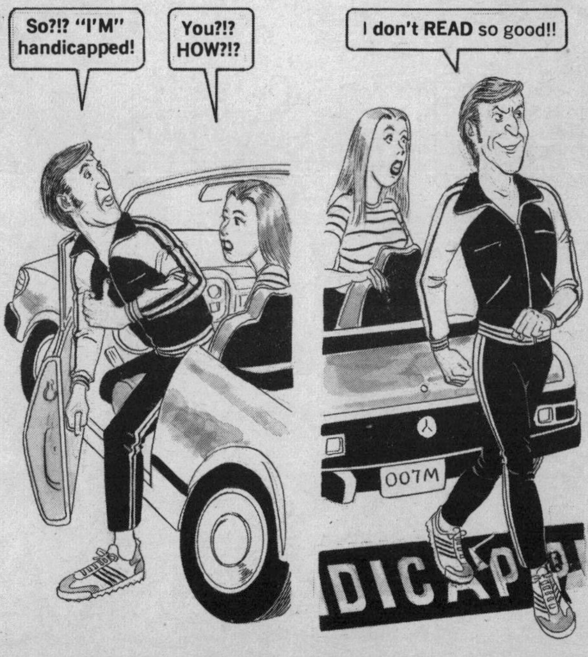
So?!? "I'M" handicapped!
You?!? HOW?!?
I don't READ so good!!
007M

GRANDPARENTS

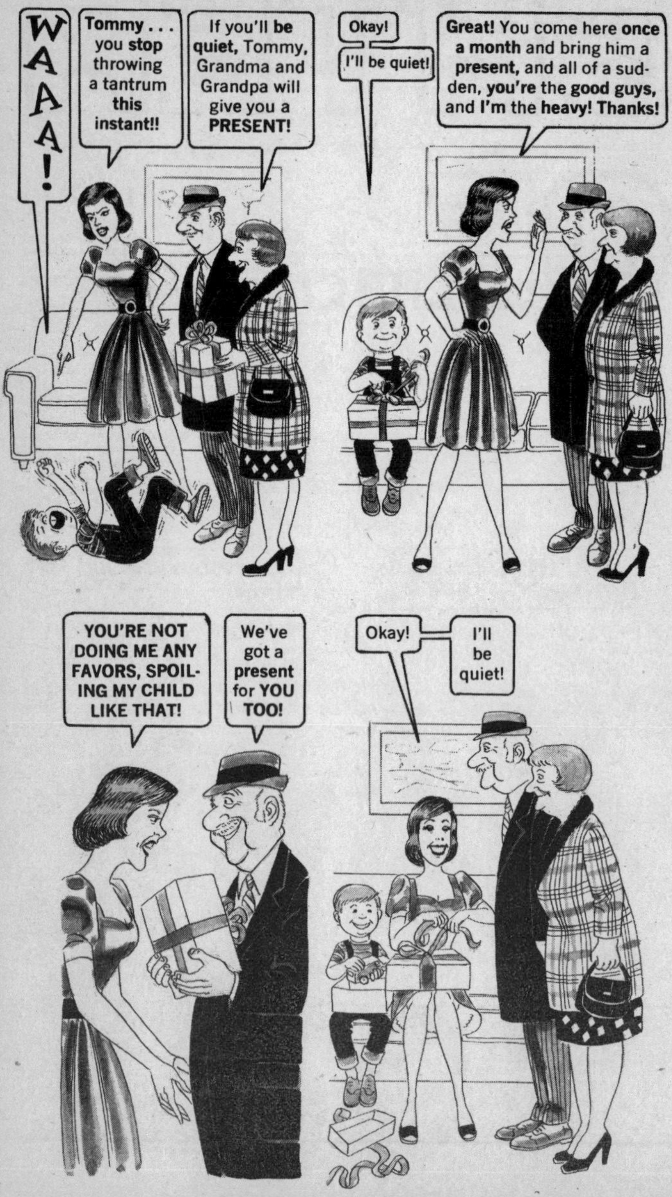
WAAA!
Tommy . . . you stop throwing a tantrum this instant!!
If you'll be quiet, Tommy, Grandma and Grandpa will give you a PRESENT!
Okay!
I'll be quiet!
Great! You come here once a month and bring him a present, and all of a sud-den, you're the good guys, and I'm the heavy! Thanks!
YOU'RE NOT DOING ME ANY FAVORS, SPOIL-ING MY CHILD LIKE THAT!
We've got a present for YOU TOO!
Okay!
I'll be quiet!

THE CAR

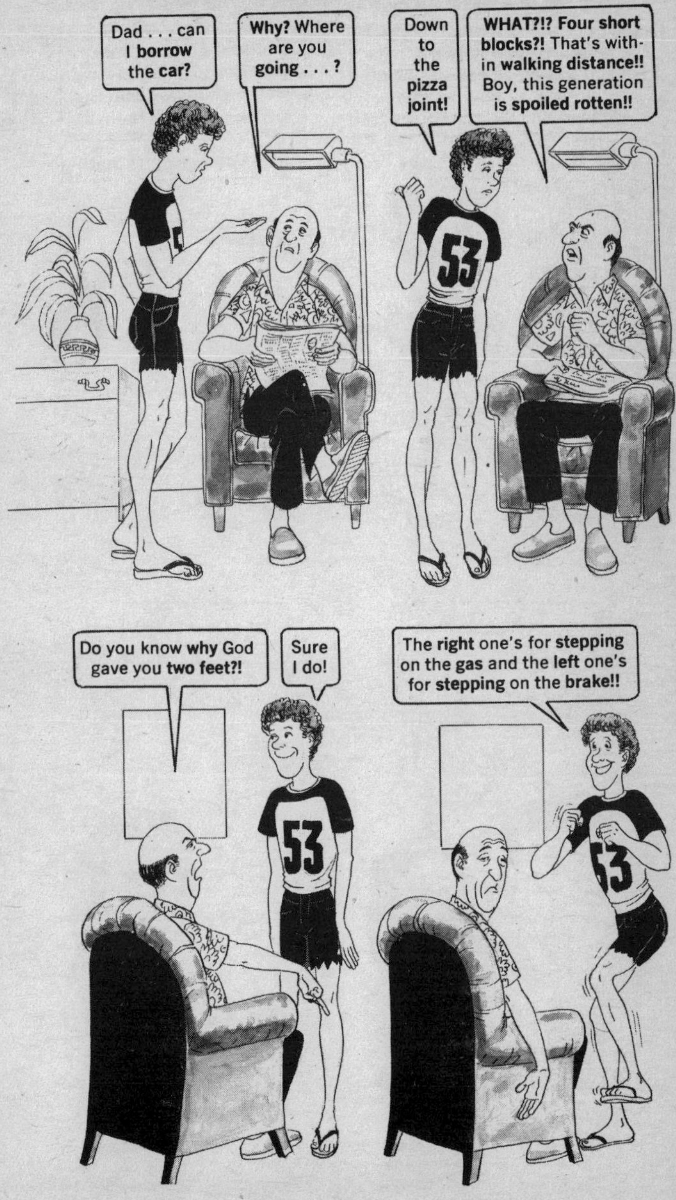

Dad . . . can I borrow the car?
Why? Where are you going . . . ?
Down to the pizza joint!
WHAT?!? Four short blocks?! That's within walking distance!! Boy, this generation is spoiled rotten!!
53
Do you know why God gave you two feet?!
Sure I do!
53
The right one's for stepping on the gas and the left one's for stepping on the brake!!
53

JOGGING

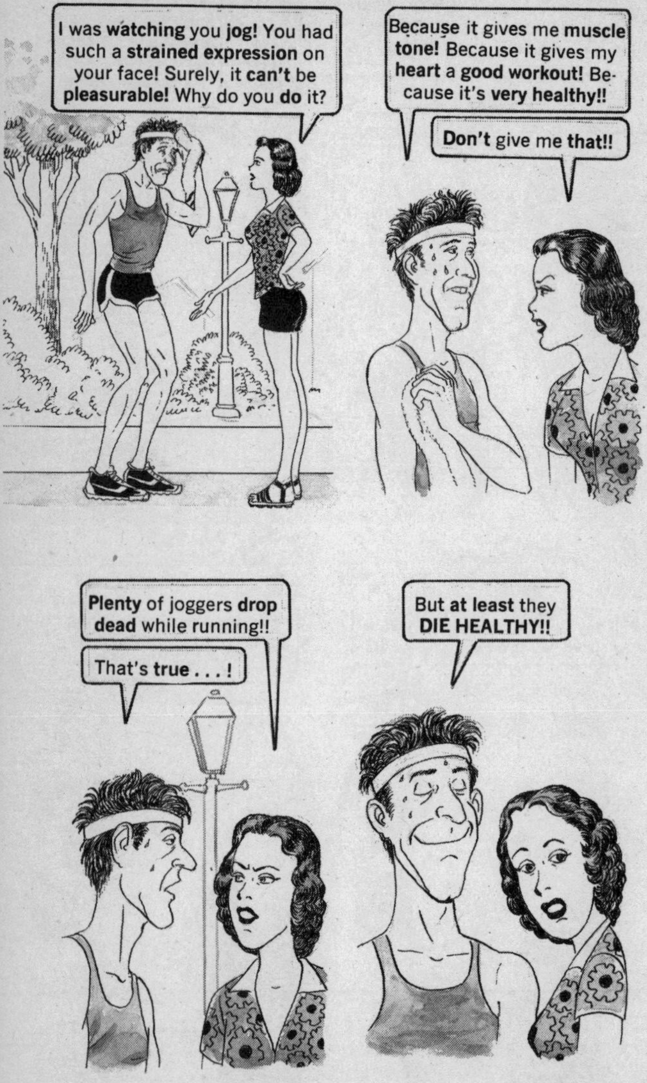
I was **watching** you **jog!** You had such a **strained expression** on your face! Surely, it **can't** be **pleasurable!** Why do you **do** it?
Because it gives me **muscle tone!** Because it gives my **heart** a **good workout!** Because it's **very healthy!!**
Don't give me **that!!**
Plenty of joggers **drop dead** while running!!
That's **true . . . !**
But **at least** they **DIE HEALTHY!!**

EATING

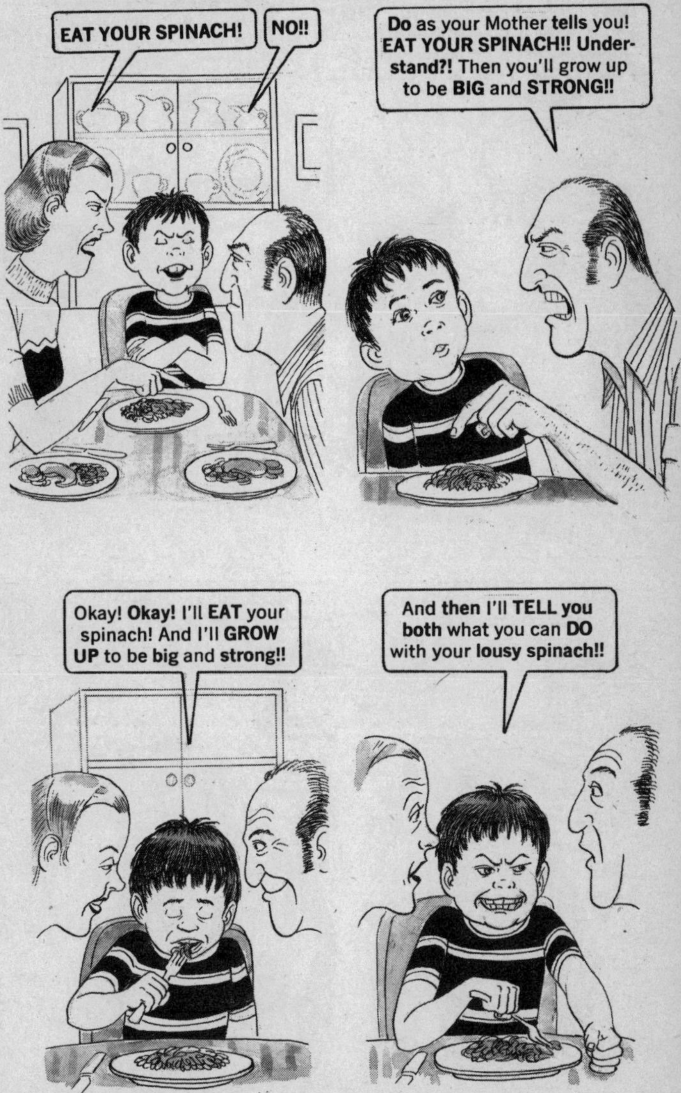

EAT YOUR SPINACH!
NO!!
Do as your Mother tells you! EAT YOUR SPINACH!! Understand?! Then you'll grow up to be BIG and STRONG!!
Okay! Okay! I'll EAT your spinach! And I'll GROW UP to be big and strong!!
And then I'll TELL you both what you can DO with your lousy spinach!!

TEENAGERS

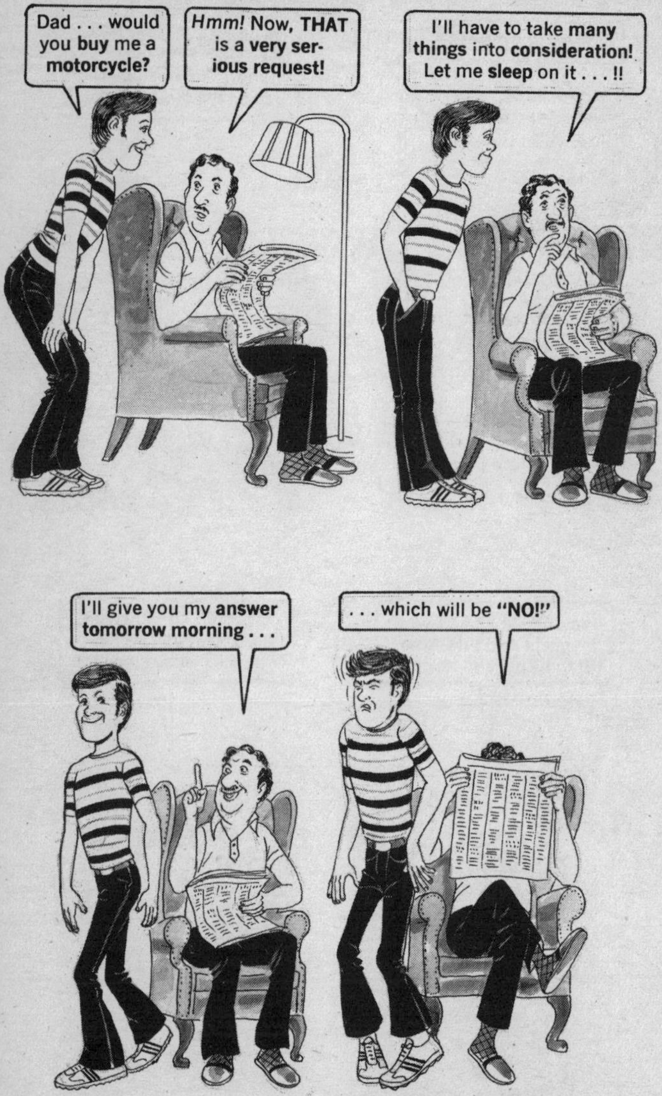

Dad . . . would you buy me a motorcycle?
Hmm! Now, THAT is a very serious request!
I'll have to take many things into consideration! Let me sleep on it . . . !!
I'll give you my answer tomorrow morning . . .
. . . which will be "NO!"

RELATIONSHIPS

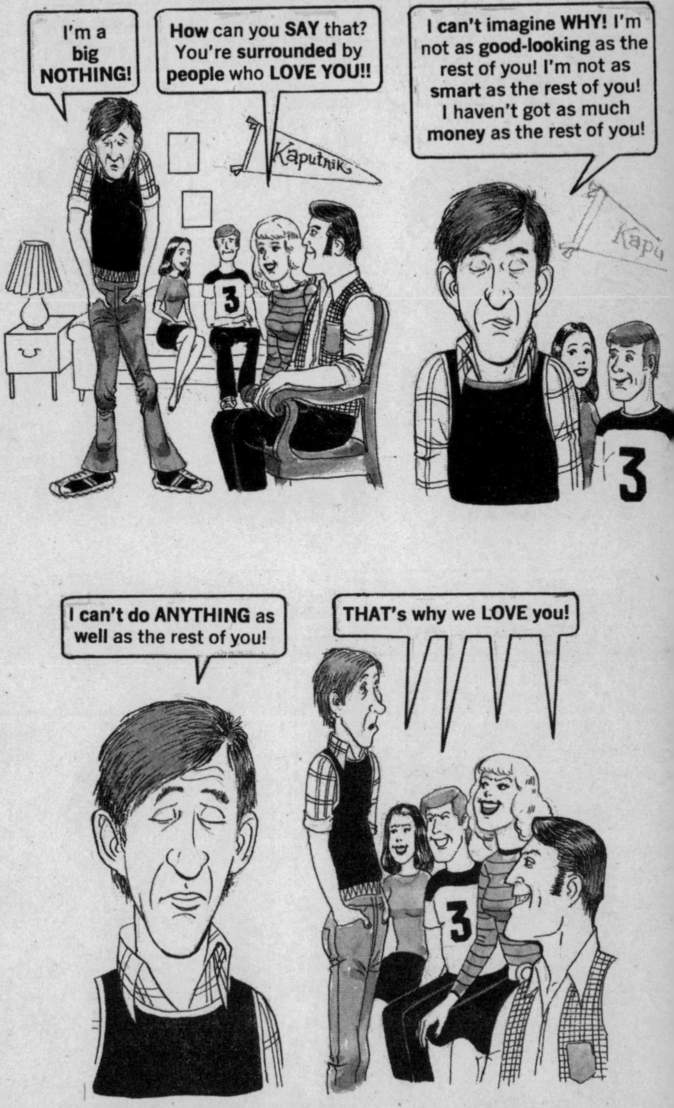
I'm a big NOTHING!
How can you SAY that? You're surrounded by people who LOVE YOU!!
Kaputnik
I can't imagine WHY! I'm not as good-looking as the rest of you! I'm not as smart as the rest of you! I haven't got as much money as the rest of you!
I can't do ANYTHING as well as the rest of you!
THAT's why we LOVE you!

THE DENTIST

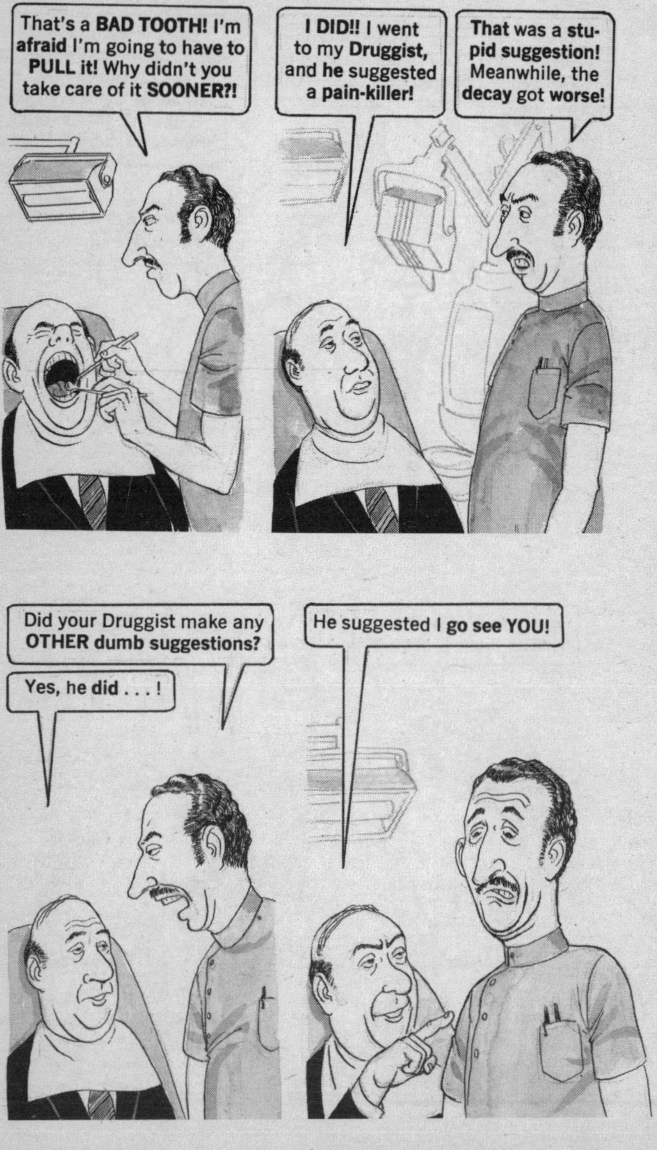
That's a BAD TOOTH! I'm afraid I'm going to have to PULL it! Why didn't you take care of it SOONER?!
I DID!! I went to my Druggist, and he suggested a pain-killer!
That was a stupid suggestion! Meanwhile, the decay got worse!
Did your Druggist make any OTHER dumb suggestions?
Yes, he did . . . !
He suggested I go see YOU!

HOSPITALITY

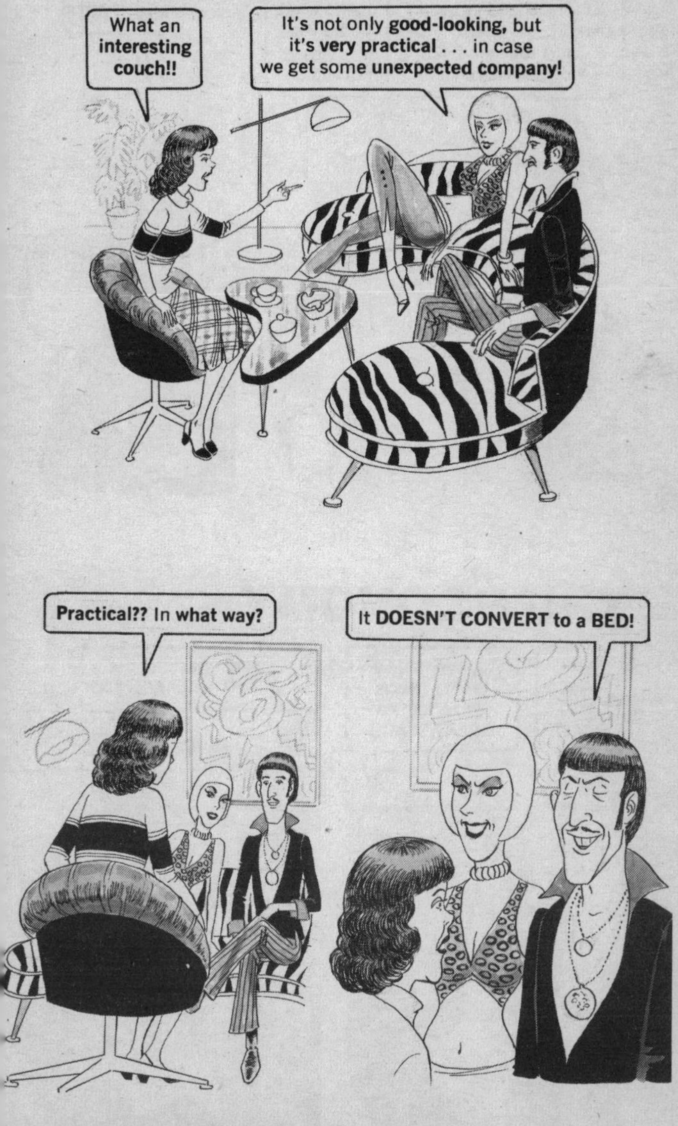

What an interesting couch!!
It's not only good-looking, but it's very practical . . . in case we get some unexpected company!
Practical?? In what way?
It DOESN'T CONVERT to a BED!

OLD FRIENDS

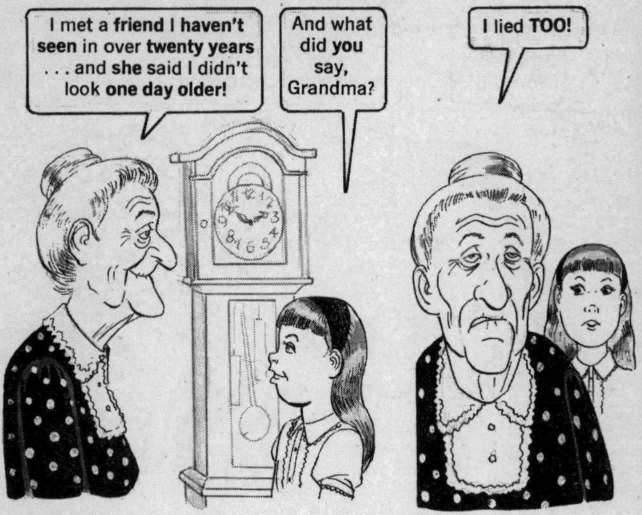
I met a friend I haven't seen in over twenty years . . . and she said I didn't look one day older!
And what did you say, Grandma?
I lied TOO!

THE ECONOMY

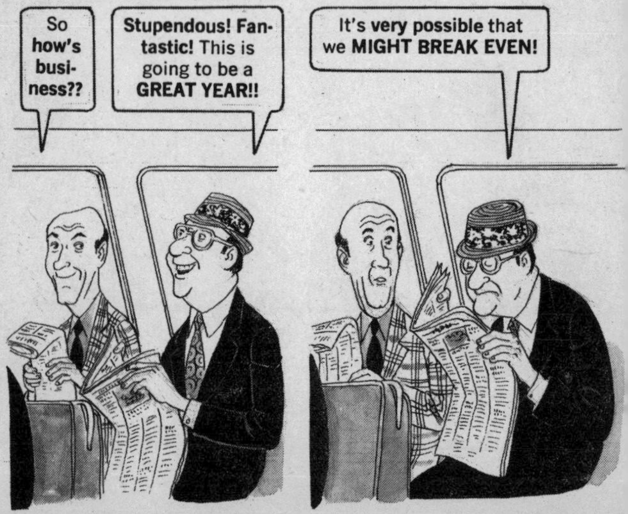
So how's busi-ness??
Stupendous! Fan-tastic! This is going to be a GREAT YEAR!!
It's very possible that we MIGHT BREAK EVEN!

REUNIONS

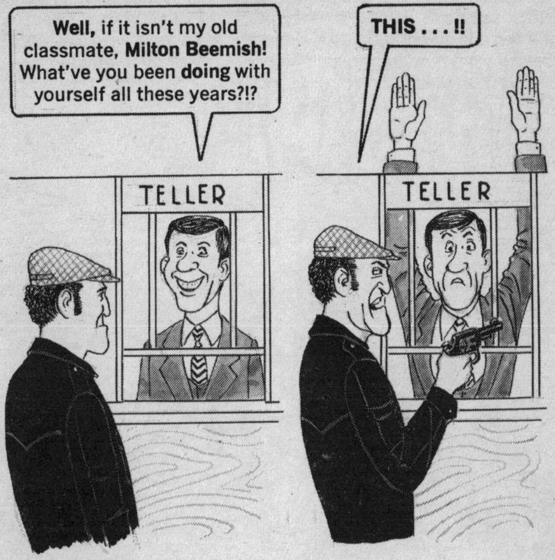
Well, if it isn't my old classmate, Milton Beemish! What've you been doing with yourself all these years?!?
TELLER
THIS . . . !!
TELLER

DANCING

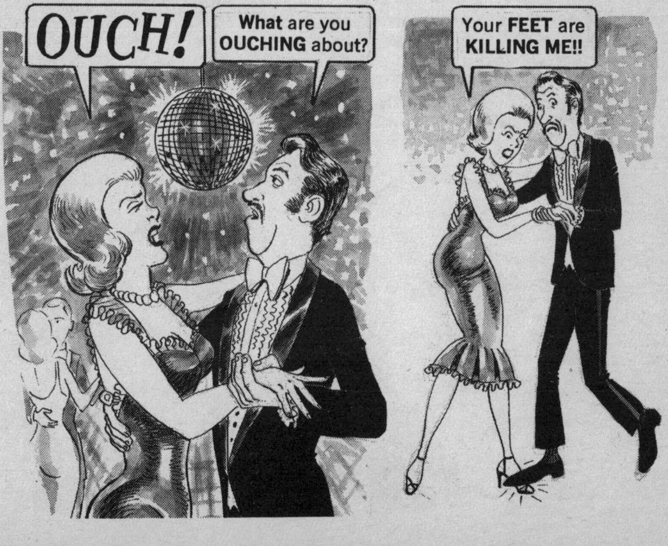
OUCH!
What are you OUCHING about?
Your FEET are KILLING ME!!

CONFESSIONS

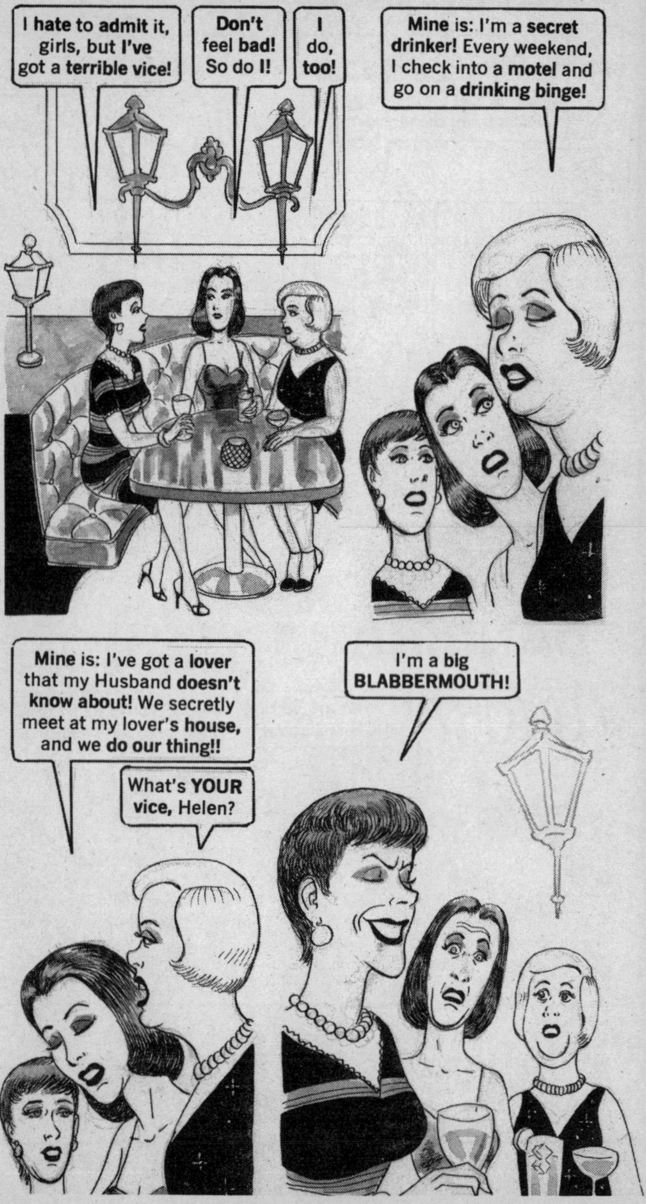
I hate to admit it, girls, but I've got a terrible vice!
Don't feel bad! So do I!
I do, too!
Mine is: I'm a secret drinker! Every weekend, I check into a motel and go on a drinking binge!
Mine is: I've got a lover that my Husband doesn't know about! We secretly meet at my lover's house, and we do our thing!!
What's YOUR vice, Helen?
I'm a big BLABBERMOUTH!

MEALS

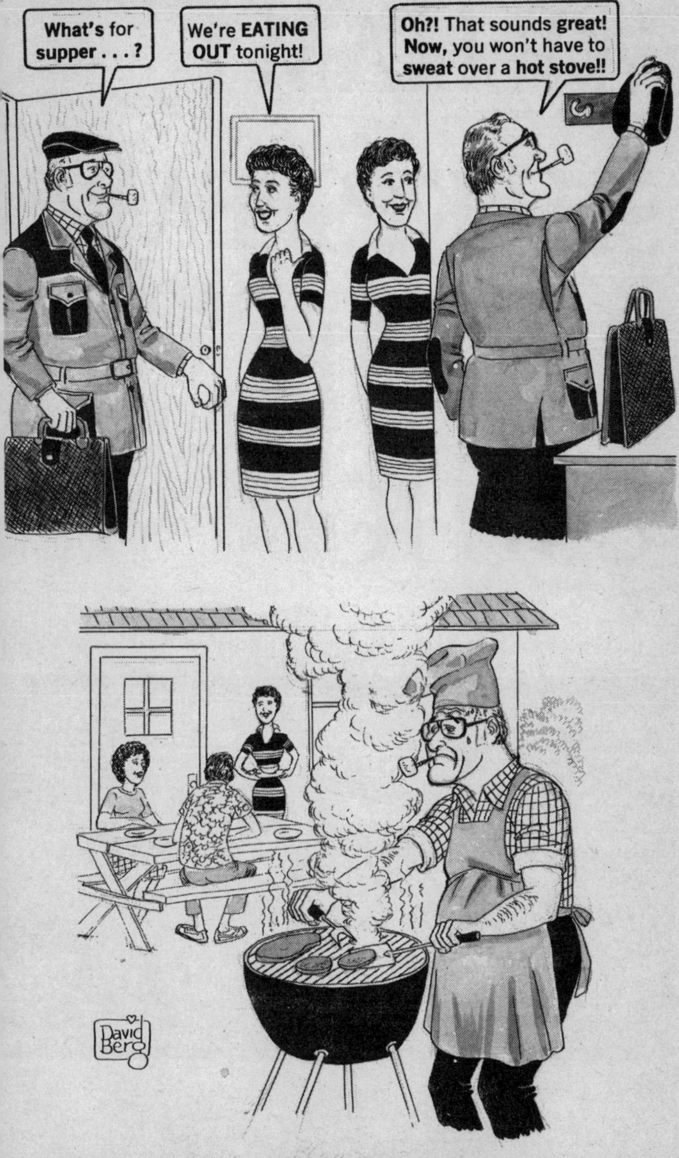
What's for supper . . . ?
We're EATING OUT tonight!
Oh?! That sounds great! Now, you won't have to sweat over a hot stove!!
David Berg

WILLIAM SHAKESPEARE ...MOVIE CRITIC

WRITER: HENRY CLARK

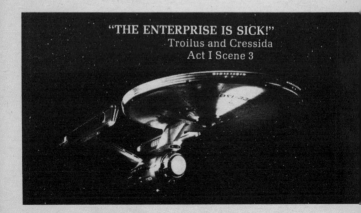

"THE ENTERPRISE IS SICK!"
Troilus and Cressida
Act I Scene 3

STAR TREK
THE MOTION PICTURE

starring
WILLIAM SHATNER

"...CAPTAIN OF THIS
RUIN'D BAND..."
Henry V
Act IV Pro.

"...WITH HIS FAT-BRAINED
FOLLOWERS SO FAR OUT..."
Henry V
Act III Scene 7

also starring
LEONARD NIMOY

"...WORN VULCAN..."
Titus Andronicus
Act II Scene 1

"...HE HAS NOT SO MUCH
BRAIN AS EAR-WAX..."
Troilus and Cressida
Act V Scene 1

and featuring
DEFOREST KELLEY & JAMES DOOHAN

"...BONES,
ILL-FAVORED..."
Henry V
Act V Scene 4

"...THE WEASEL
SCOT..."
Henry V
Act I Scene 2

"BEARS NO IMPRESSION OF THE THING AS IT WAS."
Two Gentlemen From Verona
Act II Scene 4

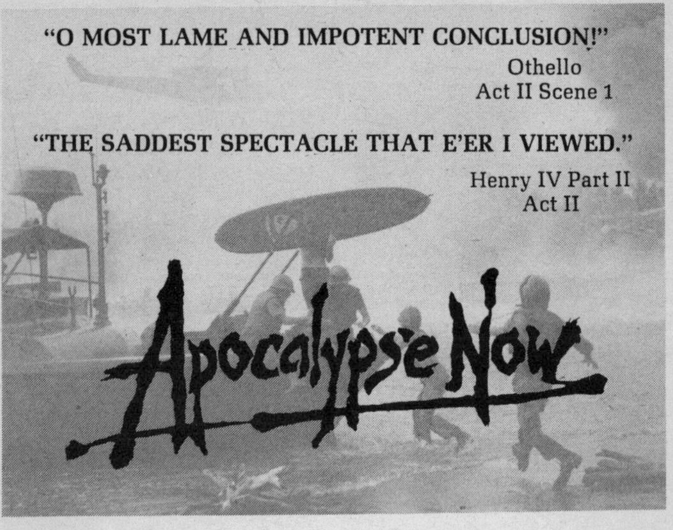
"O MOST LAME AND IMPOTENT CONCLUSION!"
Othello
Act II Scene 1
"THE SADDEST SPECTACLE THAT E'ER I VIEWED."
Henry IV Part II
Act II
Apocalypse Now

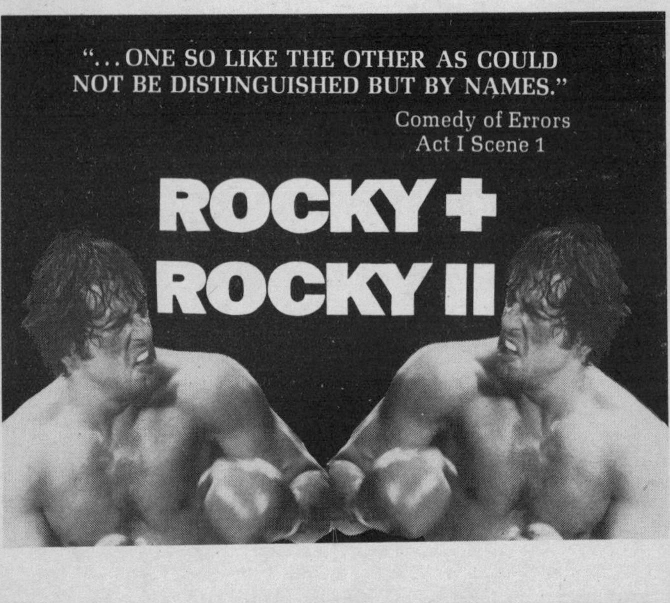
"...ONE SO LIKE THE OTHER AS COULD NOT BE DISTINGUISHED BUT BY NAMES."
Comedy of Errors
Act I Scene 1
ROCKY +
ROCKY II

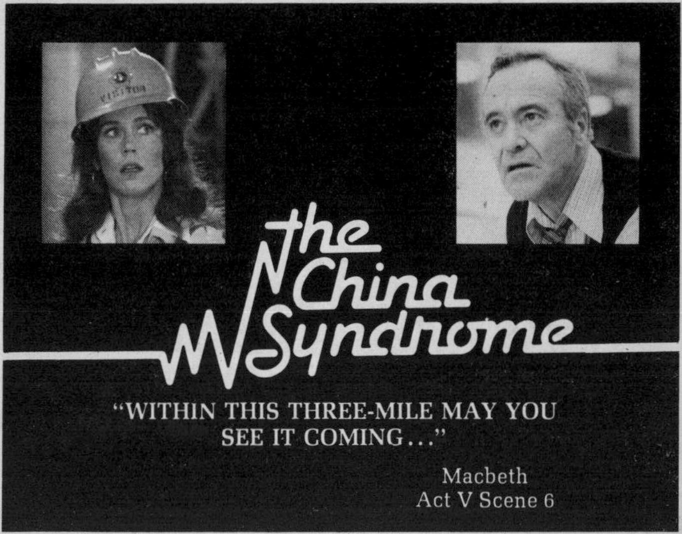
the China Syndrome
"WITHIN THIS THREE-MILE MAY YOU SEE IT COMING..."
Macbeth
Act V Scene 6

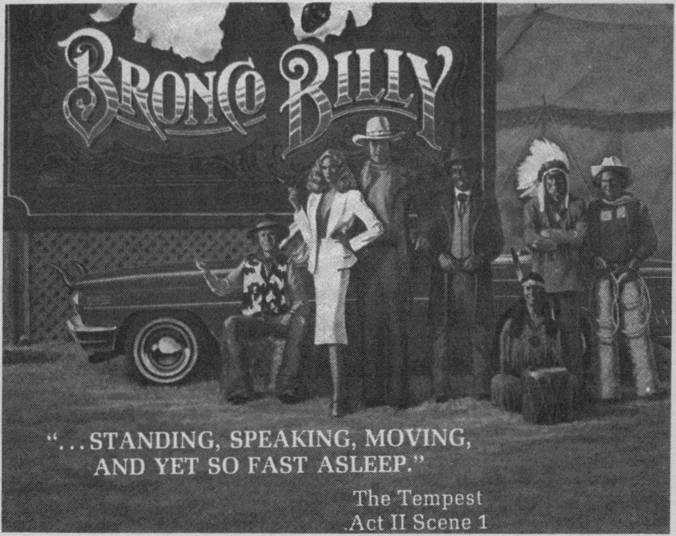
BRONCO BILLY
"...STANDING, SPEAKING, MOVING, AND YET SO FAST ASLEEP."
The Tempest
Act II Scene 1

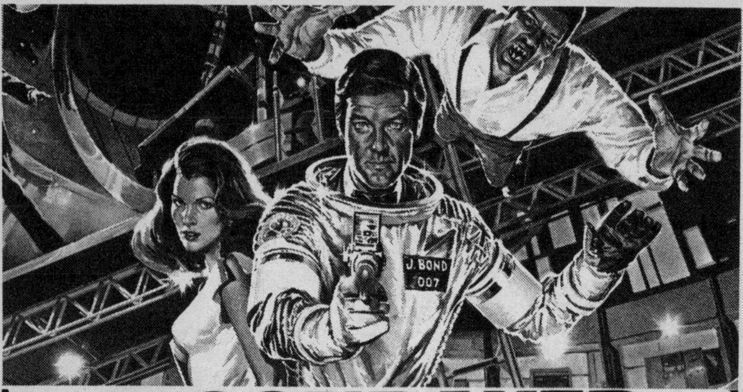
J. BOND
007

MOONRAKER

"...I PERCEIVE A WEAK BOND..."

Midsummer Night's Dream
Act III Scene 2

"...IDOL OF IDIOT-WORSHIPPERS..."

Troilus and Cressida
Act V Scene 1

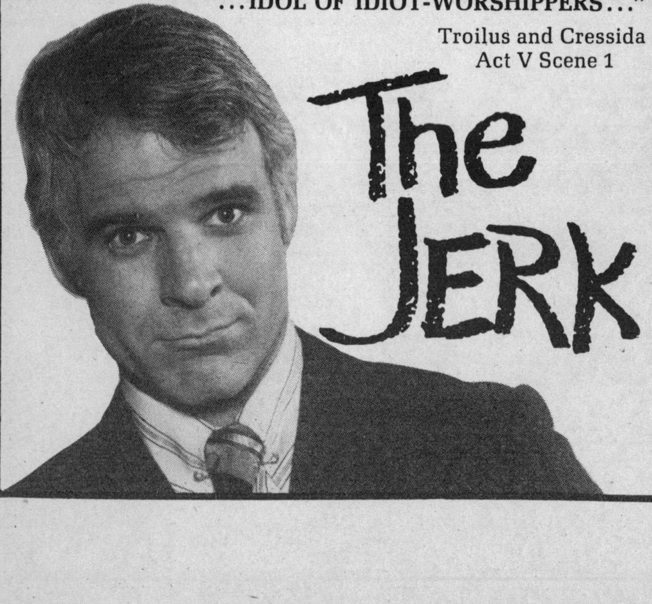
The
JERK

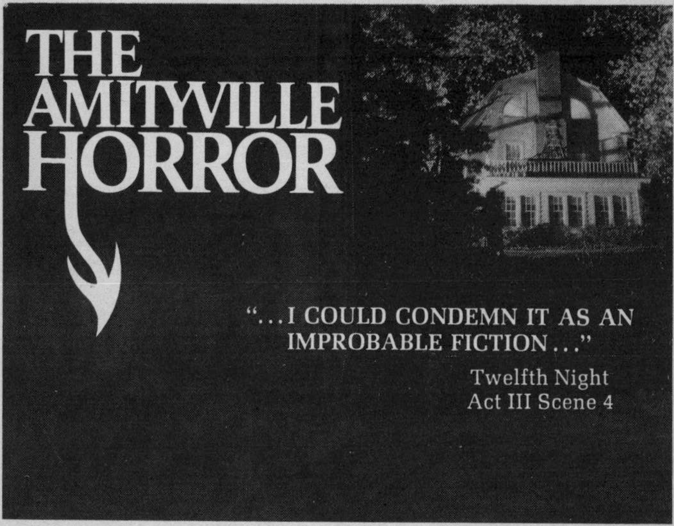
THE AMITYVILLE HORROR
"...I COULD CONDEMN IT AS AN IMPROBABLE FICTION..."
Twelfth Night
Act III Scene 4

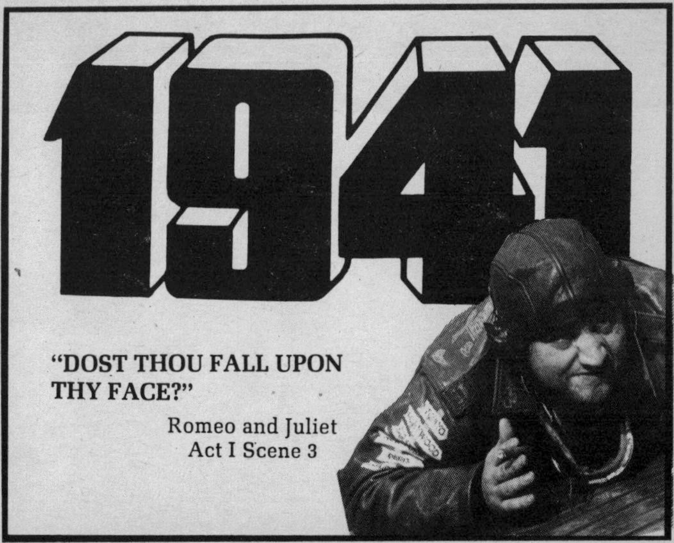
1941
"DOST THOU FALL UPON THY FACE?"
Romeo and Juliet
Act I Scene 3

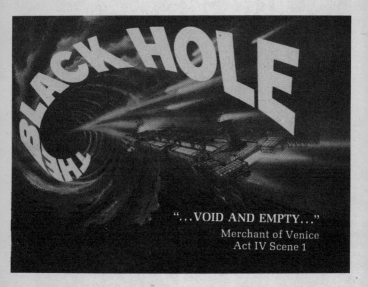

"...VOID AND EMPTY..."
Merchant of Venice
Act IV Scene 1

JOKE AND DAGGER DEPT.

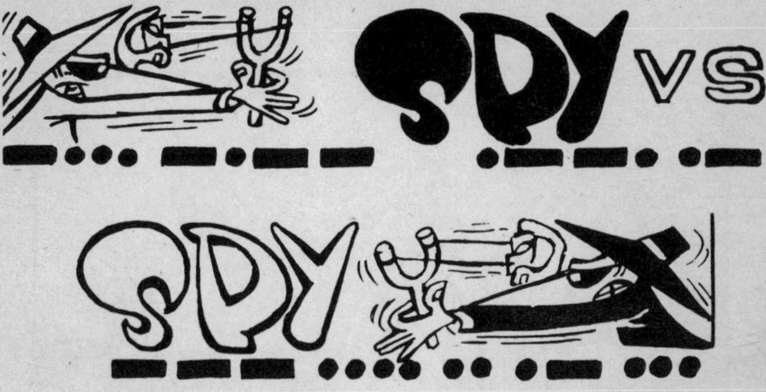
SPY VS
SPY

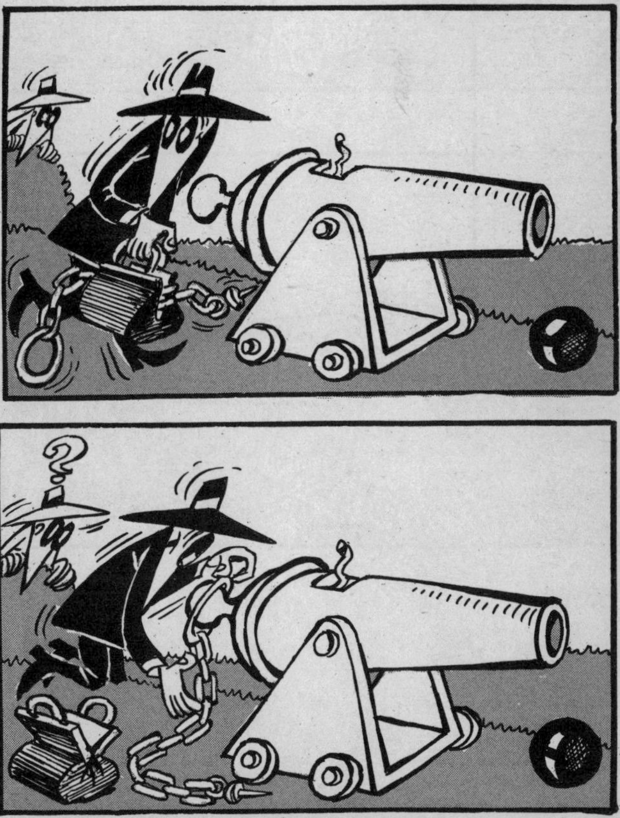

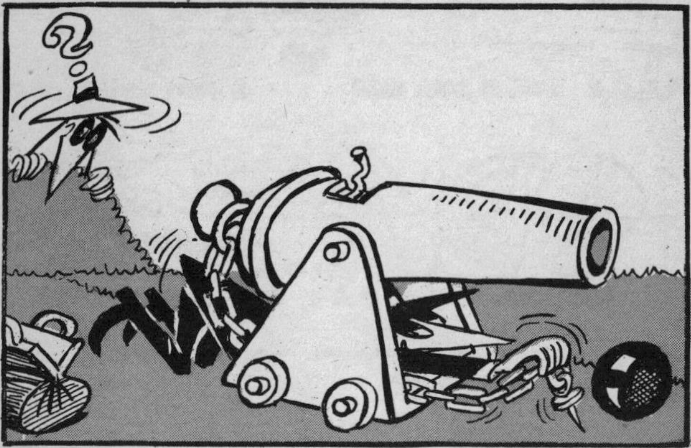
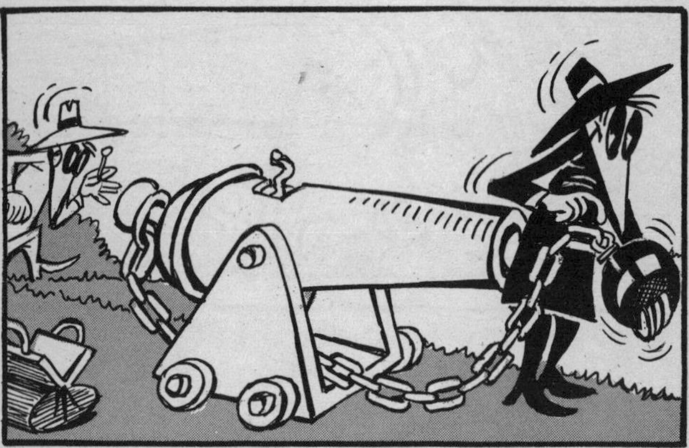

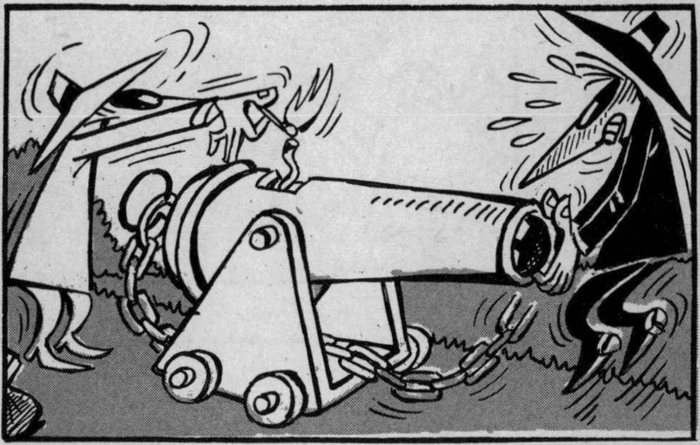

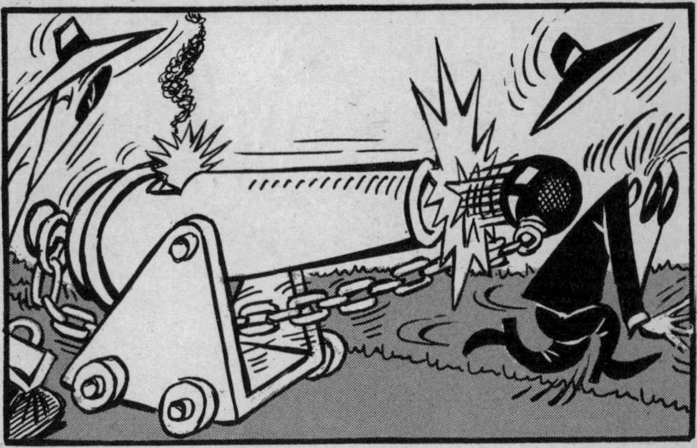